*Pembrokeshire
Look upon the land and sea
Sir Benfro*

*The inspiration for
Arts & Crafts*

Concept and Editorial: Peter Green

Celtic Horizons Publishing

Bangeston

Angle

Pembrokeshire

SA71 5AH

Tel 01646 641348

Mobile 07881 808246

Email info@celtichorizons.co.uk

www.celtichorizons.co.uk

Design & Print

Dimond Press

Pembroke

Tel 01646 682424

ISBN 0-9538352-4-3

This book has been produced with the assistance
of Pembrokeshire County Council

Contents

Preface

Pembrokeshire - Sir Benfro, county of stunning beauty and striking contrast. A source of inspiration to local and travelling artists over the centuries.

An area of 'magical and transforming light', with rugged precipitous cliffs, sweeping windswept bays surging with Atlantic swells. The everchanging Oceanic weather, with Atlantic storms of exhilarating power. Artists and craftspeople are drawn to the area, the sea is infused into their veins and they stay. The county now has an extraordinary number of artists and craftspeople. This publication celebrates the inspiration that Pembrokeshire gives to those artists and craftspeople, and the creation of inspirational works of art of extraordinary diversity.

Rhagair

Sir Benfro - sir o harddwch eithriadol a gwrthgyferbyniad trawiadol. Ffynhonnell o ysbrydoliaeth i artistiaid lleol ac artistiaid teithiol dros y canrifoedd.

Ardal o 'oleuni hudolus a thrawsnewidiol', gyda chlogwyni serth garw, cilfachau gwyllt â Môr Iwerydd yn mynd i mewn ac allan ohonynt. Y tywydd Cefnforol cyfnewidiol, â stormydd pwerus Môr Iwerydd. Caiff artistiaid a chrefftwyr eu denu i'r ardal, bydd y môr yn treiddio i'w gwythiennau a byddant yn aros. Mae gan y sir bellach nifer anhygoel

1 **Carn Llidi**
Helen Elliott
oil on canvas

2 **St Non's**
Graham Hurd-Wood
oil on canvas

o artistiaid a chrefftwyr. Mae'r cyhoeddiad hwn yn dathlu'r ysbrydoliaeth y mae Sir Benfro yn ei rhoi i'r artistiaid a'r crefftwyr hynny, a'r ddawn o greu gwaith celf ysbrydoledig yn llawn o amrywiaeth eithriadol.

Towards an Authentic Art

...Surely now there is a role for art to uplift, to echo the best in human nature, to celebrate courage, faith, humility, pride, dignity, joy and most of all our capacity to love, to care for others, the environment, the rich diversity that makes up our world. This authentic art need not be a sickly sweet choc box, the work of Mary Griffiths fulfils what is required. No page-three beauties here, but her respect (and love) for the dignity of mankind realises a deeper and fundamentally humanist beauty.

The motif, the image that provokes this sort of reaction is one that has touched us at a deeper more spiritual level than the simple pleasure of the picturesque. Peter Sculthorpe, Australia's most celebrated composer, speaks of seeking the sacred in nature as being the concern of most of his music and for that reason sometimes regards himself a religious composer.

It is far from necessity that a work of art should have a literally religious content, but a true authentic response has a spiritual quality, a quality that we all sense at our most intuitive level. When artists bring all possible forces of visual sensitivity and craftmanship revealing the essential beauty, the inner spirituality, then one can honour a true creativity that reflects our primary legacy, being made as we are told, in the image of the Divine Creator.

Extracts from the article "Towards An Authentic Art"
by Gwyn Cecil Williams.

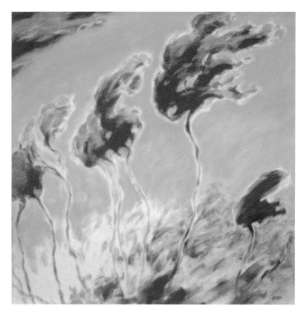

3   **Red Trees, Scolton Manor**
Gwyn Cecil Williams
24˝ x 24˝   oil/alkyd on canvas

4   **Blue Preseli Hills**
Gwyn Cecil Williams
26˝ x 26˝   oil/alkyd on canvas

Pembrokeshire -
A Sweet Seduction

From Turner to Sutherland artists have travelled to work in Pembrokeshire fascinated not only by its' beauty, but by the amazing liquid quality of its' salt washed light. The west wind blows almost continually and trees forced into arthritic submission by its' strength form pieces of living sculpture, writhing and twisting, bent almost double, adding drama to an already dramatic landscape.

From St Davids to Newport, great outcrops of rock, Carn Llidi, Pen Beri, Carn Trellwyd, Garn Fawr and others, rise from the earth like the spine of a broken backed dragon, running across North Pembrokeshire to end at Carn Ingli - Mount of Angels at the western end of the mysterious Preselis. Here ancient man came seeking spotted dolerite, quarried from Carn Meini to be transported to Salisbury Plain, for this is the famous bluestone of the inner circle of Stonehenge. The magic which drew the ancients has lost none of its' potency.

I was born here. Absorbed the riches of this giving Earth whilst still in the womb. Drank its' benison through my mother's milk. Fell under its' spell before I began to remember. Grew up on the shores of my beloved Cleddau - a truly privileged childhood.

As an artist I can do no more than paint and sculpt. Sometimes what I see but always what I feel - a direct and personal response to my mother Earth.

The coast of Pembrokeshire is justifiably famous. From the towering cliffs of Pwll Deri, where the beaches are nurseries to the grey seals, the same seals whose eerie songs are the haunting voice-of this wild place, to the

5   **Tenby Morning**
Bob Reeves
54" x 38" oils artists collection

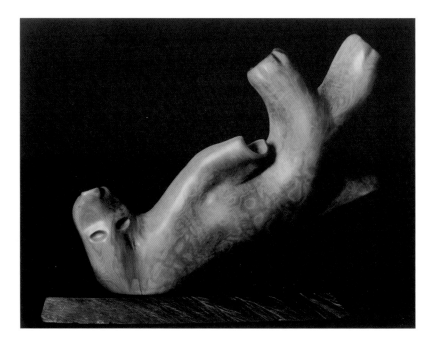

6   **Morlo**
Bob Reeves
beech and slate collection of Mrs Ann Cowie-Eynon

7 **A Dream of Annwn**
Bob Reeves
54˝ x 40˝ oils
collection of Dr & Mrs Williams, Lambourne

marram strummed and sea sculpt dunes of the great storm beach at Freshwater West, I am entranced, completely under its' spell - 'I feel my pulse and heart beat slow to share the ceaseless roaring rhythm of the restless surf. Even my breath caught, held, and then expelled to match the hissing, slow and pebble-sucking backwash, is part of this beloved hypnotism'

Who could fail to be inspired by this place? My response is immediate and personal. I am part of the circle of this Earth. Its' cycle of tides and seasons continue to entrance me. I seek no escape.

Bob Reeves, Artist, Sculptor, Poet.

The glory of Pembrokeshire is that the next stop is Mexico. The infinite stretch of Ocean, the power of it, is overwhelming compared with the charming and lovely inlets, painted by Sutherland, which are magical, but the sea is mighty.

I first began painting the sea when I was boy of fifteen in Amroth.

The sea is that which makes me aware of my own physical being.

When you get into the sea you are naked and you feel your whole body by the touch of water, especially of cold water. You have power but you are being used by a far greater power, as when you plunge into a wave. When I draw the sea it's the immense power that interests me.

I must paint on the beach. I can't remember it so I draw or paint on the beach and its very difficult in the wind and the rain. I have to get the protection of a cliff or rock to make my watercolours. In making bigger pictures of the sea, three or four feet reliefs, containing much more than can possibly included in a watercolour. I have used many drawings that I've done on shore but I don't imitate them in a larger work. I love painting to music so when I'm working in my studio I normally put on a symphony or some Bach.

8   **Rising Tide**
Arthur Giardelli
48 x 69 cms Watercolour

9   **A Pembrokeshire Thorn Tree**
Arthur Giardelli

Most of the reliefs from my first exhibition in 1965 are almost all about the sea: they show the tide coming in, wave followed by another wave, and then becoming foam as it rushes up towards the beach. That is the inspiration of the big relief sculptures and they're made, for the most part, from debris picked up on the beach or from sawn up bits of furniture.

A remarkable insight of the critic David Fraser Jenkins, is the sound that seems to emerge to him as he looks at my reliefs!

Poems often suggest the imagery for a relief or collage. I never remember which comes first, the title or the picture. I think titles often come halfway through sometimes at the end.

You will never enjoy the world aright,
till the sea itself
floweth in the your veins, till you are
clothed with the heavens,
and crowned with the stars: and
perceive yourself to be
the sole heirs as well as you...

"The Sea itself floweth in your veins", because we are animals, we are part of nature. Whatever else we may be we're certainly that.

Arthur Giardelli in conversation with
Derek Shiel. (2001 at the age of 90).

10   **A Windy Walk**
Bim Giardelli
fabric picture

11   **The Sea Has Many Voices**
Arthur Giardelli
mixed medium relief construction

12   **Moondance**
Bim Giardelli
fabric picture

13 Dinas Fach
David Bellamy
watercolour

To witness the sun pushing its golden tentacles across the south face of Everest, clouds licking their way round the vertiginous glaciers of Huascaran in the Andes, the sun setting over the Matterhorn, or the vast herds of wildebeest on the Serengeti Plain are unforgettable experiences, but for me none of those glories match the sheer beauty of the Pembrokeshire landscape. I vividly remember sketching moonbeams dancing across the tendrils of a delta thousands of feet below my campsite, and thinking such images live forever, yet how I longed to be watching great Atlantic swells hitting the rocks of Trwycynddeiriog.

David Bellamy.

14 Old Fishguard Harbour
David Bellamy
watercolour

Pembrokeshire is a land of mist and mystery, where the land meets the sea. Stories of saints and sinners are etched into the fabric of the landscape. Through many invasions and conquerors, the spirit of the people endures, in tune with nature. Eking a living from the land and sea, man has changed and shaped the landscape, but the eternal land survives.

The ethereal light and atmosphere of the Pembrokeshire coast is a magnet to artists. Combine stunning scenery

15   Barafundle Bay
Jenny Keal
pastel

16   Nevern Estuary
Jenny Keal
pastel

17   Treleddid Fawr
Jenny Keal
pastel

with a romantic Celtic history, and it weaves an irresistible spell to enchant us all.

Jenny Keal.

Jenny Keal draws her inspiration from the rich history of man's relationship with the landscape, scarred by industry and shaped by farming: a landscape sculpted by human activity as well as nature.

Her special interest is in vernacular architecture and social history and she is content to explore the most remote places, often on foot, sometimes on horseback or cycling to locate an old farm or cottage set in wild scenery. The historical associations have a profound influence on her work, motivating her to portray how history has a powerful effect on the landscape and the way we see it. Her inspiration is also drawn from the atmospheric effects of the weather on the landscape and the intricate geology of mountains, valleys and coast. She frequently travels in the British Isles, especially in the Celtic fringe, in search of natural landscapes and the local vernacular architecture, making a particular study of the similarities and differences in the cultures.

Creativity, if it has any meaningful boundary, lies within the moment when potential begins to emerge into reality. As that process begins to be articulated the seeds of art are sown.

Most of us share the seeds of other's work - we see their art and begin to share their creativity. There then begins the feeding of our own latent creativity, which is so essential to the full development of our humanity; we can escape the boundaries imposed upon us by our intellectual and physical dependencies.

What follows is an insight into the work of one who has devoted his life to developing his creativity and experiencing it so that we can all be fed.

Robin Bradbury writing on the work of John Knapp-Fisher.

My methods of working, and the subjects I like to paint have changed little in the forty five years since I resolved to make a living from my art.

Any changes have been the result of perfecting technique, evolvement and refinement. I work - and have always worked, in the initial stages at least, direct from my subject - direct from nature.

Many people say I do not use much colour. This is not correct, for although I do have a limited palette, I am seeking what I call 'the edge of colour', where the earth colours and touches of primary colour emerge from the dark and where tonal relationships, quality, texture and chiaroscuro are all important.

My subjects continue to be landscape, seascape, buildings, boats, figures, animals and fish. I observe, feel and interpret. I do not copy. Nor do I invent, which is why I am not an abstract painter in the accepted definition of the term.

I aim to produce pictures that are exciting, have strong compositional form and powerful visual imagery.

John Knapp-Fisher (taken from a statement on his art).

18 Deraints Cottage
John Knapp-Fisher
oil 2002

19   Shore
John Knapp-Fisher
oil 2002

20   **Evening Showers**
      Annabel Greenhalgh
      pastel

21   **Passing Snow**
      Annabel Greenhalgh
      pastel

22   **Summer's Evening, Freshwater West**
      Annabel Greenhalgh
      pastel

I fell in love with Pembrokeshire twenty years ago and decided to stay. I had come home.

My artistic background started with drawing in pencil and charcoal from a very young age and then being totally captivated by my first visit to the Uffizi in Florence at the age of 12. I started to study the work of the Great Masters. Charcoal naturally led to pastel and this is now my chosen medium as it has a density of colour which gives me the depth and solidity I need for my work.

I draw emotional strength and well being from my environment and aim to convey this pleasure and excitement through my landscapes.

From Preseli storms and coastal walks to crashing waves and summer beaches. Pembrokeshire holds the magic of it all.

Annabel Greenhalgh

23 **Path To Druidston**
Annabel Greenhalgh
pastel

24　Garnllwŷd, near Abereiddy
John Rogers
12˝ x 24˝ watercolour

The wonderful lichen-covered slabs of rock on the Pembrokeshire coast remind me of the work of Serge Poliakoff and De Stijl. The broad landscape swings my thoughts like a pendulum to the artists of seventeenth-century Holland and to the 'plein air' Impressionists; to Courbet, and back to Chinese painters of the Sung period.

Before I moved to St. Davids, Pembrokeshire, to devote all my time to painting (and where I opened my own gallery in 1972) I found the contemporary milieu alien to my ideas of painting the landscape in situ. Convinced however, that at least my works would be genuine workman-like observations of place and time, I persevered. I must have been justified, since nowadays many young professionals take their easels outside.

I came early on the problem of realism and equally early abandoned the idea of pure objectivity. Finding my own solutions to a continual stream of technical problems, I gradually evolved a personal visual language.

I try to paint Genius Loci, the spirit of place: visual poems engendered by the experience of

25　Caerlem Farm, Garn Fawr, Strumble
John Rogers
14" x 32" watercolour

being and working in a particular place at a particular time. Some subjects I have drawn and painted over and over again from various perspectives, through all seasons and times of day. The results are like looking into the faces of old friends rather than snapshots of strangers.

Great landscape painters of the past like William Turner expressed a concept of the world quite different from ours. We can fly to the moon and dive beneath oceans, we know that microscopic imbalance in the eco-system can have far reaching consequences. We have witnessed the splitting of the atom and the devastation that followed. We understand our planet in a way unique to our time.

Our concern for the conservation of wild places and the balance of nature makes landscape painting important again. I hope that my work will contribute to the growing awareness of how vulnerable our planet is, and the great beauty and mystery it stores for us all and future generations.

John Rogers

The Tenby Museum and Art Gallery exhibition 'Tenby through the Artist's Eye', illustrates the way in which the unique beauty of the landscape of the Tenby area has been depicted throughout the centuries by artists of varying styles. The wide ranging collection of paintings, drawings and prints on display reflects the changing fashion of art throughout the centuries and the exhibition includes the work of some artists of world renown, such as JMW Turner, Gwen John and Lucian Freud and other artists who have lived in the area and devoted their lives to recording the local scene, together with the work of artists who have visited Tenby for brief periods. This exhibition includes work by both experienced professional artists and by enthusiastic and accomplished amateurs. The works selected provide an historical and topographical record of Tenby across the centuries, illustrating how the charm and the beauty of the locality has attracted and continues to attract artists of considerable merit.

Extract taken from the statement by John Beynon, Honourary Curator, Tenby Museum and Art Gallery.

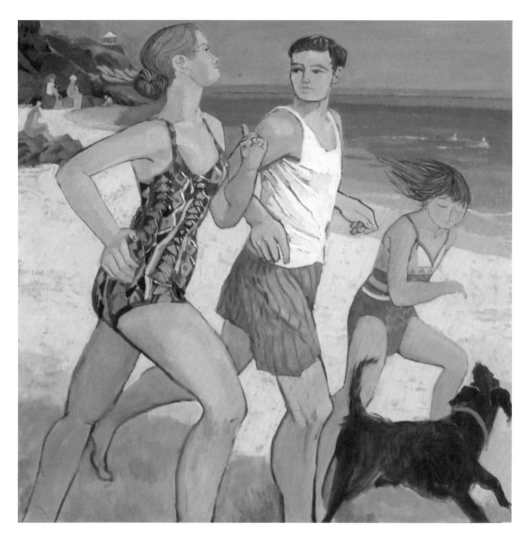

26   Running with the dog
Claudia Williams
80 x 80 cm oil on canvas 2002

I love the different view points and eye levels here and of course it is often busy with people enjoying the seaside. So it gives me plenty of ideas for one of my favourite subjects, Bathers.

Claudia Williams

27 Tenby Harbour
Gwilym Prichard
52 x 73 cm oil on canvas 2001

28 Cliffs and Sea Thrift
Gwilym Prichard
73 x 53 cms oil on canvas 2001

The area requires a more colourful palette than north Wales. There is a different quality to the light, more akin to Brittany where we lived for 16 years. The landscape in Pembrokeshire is broken by wind bent elm trees, dense dark thorn trees and rocky hills that appear to be mountains because of the scale. The coastal cliffs, sea thrift slopes and the ever changing sea add excitement and colour. During all the seasons - Tenby - the harbour, houses and beaches constantly change in response to the weather: storms giving way to brilliant blue sky and cotton wool clouds.

Gwilym Prichard

29 St Govan's Head
Naomi Tydeman
5″ x 5″ watercolour

'As with many artists, light is the motivation behind most of my paintings and quite often the subject matter becomes secondary. I love the effects of light that can be achieved with watercolours and how magical and evocative they can be, but also their seeming independence and self will. I do not believe there are any rules in watercolours and like to mix traditional techniques with contemporary approaches - and see what happens.'

Naomi Tydeman

30 Vestry, Gumfreston Church
Naomi Tydeman
14″ x 21″ watercolour

31   **Druidstone**
Naomi Tydeman
4˝ x 10˝ watercolour

32   **Tenby Skyline**
Naomi Tydeman
6˝ x 12˝ watercolour

33   Manorbier Castle, November
John Cahill
gouache

35   Tenby Harbour
David Morgan
watercolour

34   Ebb Tide (Tenby)
John Cahill
oil

'Most of my work depicts the rural and coastal landscape of Pembrokeshire, usually within about 20 miles of Tenby. The location is so inspiring that an artist wouldn't need to travel too far for subject matter. The landscape pictures are all based on particular views but I often change to suit my own ideas. The paintings often start off with the composition, I start to work on the textures and details using many different techniques which are both descriptive and decorative.'

John Cahill

36   **Penberri from Tretio**
Jan Gregson
mixed media

My work has evolved from a lifelong interest in art and nature. Moving to Pembrokeshire from the industrial north in the 1970's sparked off the desire to understand and paint the unique diversity of landscape available. From landscape to seascape. hidden cottages. working farms. and the Preseli Hills all changing with the seasons. weather. light and dramatic skies.

Watercolour has traditionally been my primary media. the fluidity. clarity and unpredictability complimenting the nature of Pembrokeshire.

Jan Gregson

Pembrokeshire... A focal point for contemporary Welsh Landscape.

"...it was in this area that I learned that landscape was not necessarily scenic, but that its parts have an individual figurative detachment. I found that this was equally true of other places which I visited later: but the clear, yet intricate construction of the landscape of the earlier experience, coupled with an emotional feeling of being on the brink of some drama, taught me a lesson and had an unmistakable message that has influenced me profoundly!"

This statement by the major British artist Graham Sutherland formed part of an article entitled 'Welsh Sketchbook' (Horizon, 28th April, 1942) and it attests to the importance he places, for the development of his vision, on his first visit to Wales in 1934. The area that was so vital for the development of his unique mood of landscape style was of course Pembrokeshire.

Surrounded almost on all sides by the mirror of the sea and with little industrial or urban air pollution, this county is renowned for its quality of light. Pembrokeshire light has a special luminosity that enhances colour and continues to promote exuberance amongst most sensitive artists, but especially painters. Because it is a coastal area in the far west of the British Isles, the effects of rain, wind and storm are paramount in the moulding of the landscape. Everywhere one sees the evidence of the elemental forces, in the pattern of growth, the erosion of ancient stones or the shaping of a wind-sculptured thorn tree.

37 Newgale Low Water
Maggie Driscoll Williams
21˝ x 22˝ Acrylic on Fabriano paper

38 Summer in the Preseli's
Gwyn Cecil Williams
26˝ x 26˝ Oil/Alkyd on Canvas

39   Red Algae
Maggie Driscoll Williams
21˝ x 22˝ Acrylic on Fabriano Paper

40   Spring Gorse
Maggie Driscoll Williams
21˝ x 22˝ Acrylic on Fabriano Paper

It was perhaps. Sutherland who first found the expressive force in these. the aerodynamically deformed and ubiquitous flora of the Pembrokeshire hedgerow. Among it's cruel thorns he found the visual metaphor for the cruelty of man: a cruelty that informed the images for his Nottingham Crucifixion.

It would be difficult for the majority of contemporary landscape painters to proclaim Sutherland as a direct precursor. and yet the wind-sculptured thorn tree has become a modern-day icon. It occurs in a variety of forms and is to many artists an acceptable motif. It is a motif that is symbolic of a deeper and less sentimental understanding of the force of nature.

Current trends regularly react against . rather than continue. the tradition of a previous form. What is evident. however. is how regularly. when practitioners find art in one of its frequent troughs. the path to rebirth and deeper insight is found in a return to the study of nature.

The integrity of a work of art can be consistently judged by the depth of emotion stimulated in the artist by his sensitivity to the visual world. Sutherland talks of the shiver down the spine that proves the validity of the visual encounter. The serious. innovative landscape painters of today are not merely reactionaries trying to recapture the heady days of the late nineteenth century. Surely the role of an artist was always to re-invent in modern terms the art of the past and in doing so give it significance for the future.

That Pembrokeshire commands a position on the high ground of Welsh art can only be doubted by those whose lack of perception blinds them to the County's pre-eminence.

Extracts from the article "Pembrokeshire - a focal point for contemporary Welsh Landscape". by Gwyn Cecil Williams.

'Nid oes tecach tir Ynys y Cedyrn...'

It is no secret to anyone who has visited Pembrokeshire that it's coastline is one of the most beautiful in the world. But one needs to know the place, from winter through to winter, year in, year out, to grasp something other than a superficial recognition of its beauty.

Linda Norris has learnt to speak Welsh and to draw respectful inspiration from the elements that form the landscape, the seascape and the people around her. She is conscious, at dusk and at all times 'of the spilled blood that went to the making of the wild sky'[1]. She has seen the 'meanings' in 'that certain slant of light'[2], which the wondrous Pembrokeshire skies throw out on the shiny grey of its cromlechi; its black crags and the blue-straw that is its green-grass.

To catch one of her paintings within one's field of vision is to taste the salt, feel the wind and loose ones soul in the breathtaking outdoors that is the coast of Pembrokeshire.

41 **Dark Boundary**
Linda Norris
20 x 40 cm mixed media 2002

The paradox of this almost Atlantic coastline - at once a beginning and an end, a menacing threat and a peaceful welcome - is palpable in Linda's most recent collection. It offers an uneasy beauty, even the gold of the gorse and the purple of the heather that surprise the eye in her skies and seas, are rough to the touch. They endure the elements and resist all efforts to uproot them.

'Gwydn' - tenacious, 'garw' - coarse, extreme; these are the adjectives that come to the mind held by the spell of this work. And free. Watching her paintings, one can inhale this freedom - if only temporarily. There is rebellion here that is not a romanticised notion alone of life in this Mabinogionland - but one that realises what it is to become Welsh, to live in west Wales today.

If the collection is called 'Wild Coast', the titles of the individual paintings make one aware of the central role of the sky in the work. It is the broad canvas of the sky that has given Linda's imagination the means to escape. In this latest collection, the careful delineation of her well-learned craft and the earlier controlled observance of detailed imitation has given way to a spirit that is impressionistic, now bold, now gentle, now confrontational, now in humble awe of the forces around her.

These Pembrokeshire paintings are not the place itself: they are the emotions of the place. These are not the recreation of the detail of a certain moment: they are the evocation of a moment. This work is an interpretation, each piece a poem of a painting.

Mererid Hopwood

1. R.S. Thomas (1952) From his poem 'Welsh Landscape',
Collected Poems. London: Collins.

2. Emily Dickenson from her poem 'A Certain Slant of Light'

42　**Gusting Cloud**
Linda Norris
20 x 20 cm mixed media 2002

Manorbier

The sky is filled with birds. They swoop in and out of the tree tops, just as they dive and swirl in full colour upon the canvas of Philip Sutton's paintings.

'Imagine a tree that grows on a cliff top bent over by the prevailing winds. That same tree planted somewhere else would be a different shape. The tree responds to the winds upon the cliff as human beings respond to what is around them. If I was in a different situation, my work would be different. It is an unconscious difference though. I am not aware of the effect my surroundings have on me any more than I am aware of being older each day and each week' says Philip.

The Pembrokeshire home which he shares with his wife Heather has all the colour and life of one of his paintings. It is here each morning that they rise to a distant sea crashing upon the shores of Manorbier. From the blue porch,

43 **Crows Over Manorbier**
Philip Sutton
72˝ x 72˝ oil on canvas 1990-91

with its huge jugs and vases full of flowers and green shrubs, one steps into a garden, rambling now with the early blooms of Spring. A plum tree stands sprinkled in pink blossom, and a richly scented Rosemary plant sprouts mauve flowers. The garden is the work of Heather and many of Sutton's paintings reflect the flowers she grows here.

In the field beyond the garden a white horse grazes, unaware that it has caught Philip's imagination and has become the focus for some of his paintings. A well trodden path leads to a wooden gate in a leaning wall. Pass into a hidden woodland. Spring foliage carpets the ground. This magical place and the coastal paths of Pembrokeshire provide Sutton with his ever changing canvas.

Jane Baker.

44　**The Pembroke Coast**
Philip Sutton
40″ x 40″ oil on canvas 1989

My main interest is working from life inside or outside. A spontaneous reaction to the subject, I believe can only be achieved on the spot and avoids the mechanical rendering of the subject which occurs when the artist relies on copying from photographic material which produces an image frozen in time devoid of change of movement or light.

Sitting down outside probably not in great comfort, the light and weather changing by the minute, you can see 360 degrees but you must focus on what you want and record it quickly. An artist friends comment I actually remember was 'Setting the pinger crystalizes the mind'.

The image required must be focused in the mind as the artist works. This sometime, impressionistic feel to my work is a comment perhaps an unfinished statement re. the subject, leaving something for the imagination of the viewer, but the adrenaline, excitement and determination, are what will eventually produce the results. They will produce disappointment but the successes are the achievement of the artist working 'en plein air' from life.

Vanessa Pearson

45   Pembroke Castle
Vanessa Pearson
pastel

46   Primroses
Vanessa Pearson
watercolour

47   Angle Farm
Vanessa Pearson
pastel

48 Vale of Angle
Vanessa Pearson
pastel

49 Sleeping Sheep
Vanessa Pearson
oil

50 Preseli
Vanessa Pearson
pastel

51　Sunset over Skomer
Ann Whalley
pastel

For those with a love of natural beauty and a desire to record it while at the same time improving their painting skills, then Pembrokeshire has everything to offer. We have a magnificent coastline of huge cliffs and wide beaches, tidal rivers, rolling mountains, ancient castles and pretty villages. Pembrokeshire also boasts an equable, warm and sunny climate, with a clear sparkling light to enhance the landscape.

Haroldston (an old Viking name!) has been our home for over thirty years. This is where our four sons roamed on their ponies, and built their dens and rafts in peaceful safety, which still continues. The present house dates, in part, from somewhere in the 1750's, not grand but substantial and greatly loved. It stands beside an ancient bridge that crosses the Merlin Brook close to its confluence with the Western Cleddau, which ultimately becomes the Milford Haven. What was once a paddock for ponies is now Theo's hillside garden full of plants, which he has brought home from the Mediterranean countries, as well as carefully conserved local species. Here our guests can paint at ease in undisturbed tranquillity. We are situated in the centre of the County and therefore within a short drive of any number of wonderful painting venues-beautiful gardens, historic buildings, and a huge area of unspoiled coastline and countryside.

Ann Whalley

52   **Druidstone Haven**
Theo Whalley
pastel

Pembrokeshire is a place you never tire of. and has been the starting point of all my work. I love its' everchanging moods through the seasons. the sudden changes from brilliant light to mysterious mists and shade. the heart-stopping glory of sunrise and sunset. This richness of atmospheric phenomena seduces me and is the basis of my painting. There is a splendid untamed wildness in the rocks and stones. in the crashing seas and violent skies. which are an unending stimulation. I spend many hours wandering the cliffs and hills absorbing their stark beauty - there is nothing tame or nice about this ancient land and I think that over the years it has become a part of me.

Theo Whalley

53 Little Haven
Simon Swinfield
watercolour

54 Boats at Solva
Simon Swinfield
watercolour

Having spent many idyllic childhood summer holidays in Pembrokeshire, Simon Swinfield returned to begin professionally painting here in 1994.

His paintings are to be found in all corners of the world from Finland to New Zealand, his atmospheric and figurative watercolours distil the diverse moods, depth of light and rich sky colours unique to the Pembrokeshire coastline captured in all seasons.

Simon's love of the ocean is reflected in his subject matter and local working boats are characteristic of many of his paintings particularly the infamous Solva fishing boat 'The Vital Spark'!

There is a summer exhibition at The Chapel by the Sea Gallery in Nolton Haven and various art outlets in the county.

Simon Swinfield

55   The Coast Road
Simon Swinfield
watercolour

56 **Birdlife, Pembrokeshire**
Anna Kirk-Smith
24″ x 48″ acrylic 2001

Pembrokeshire to me is the rhythmical crashing of waves and the chattering of choughs, the flaming gorse twisted with antiquity and the stones solid with it. It is a landscape embued with a weighty history, its rocks speak of myths and legends.

I am unceasingly fascinated by the marine patterns, the unexpected life revealed by the tidal cycle and the geological formations standing as monuments to erosion through the centuries. It is a county with layer upon layer of visual poetry to be explored.

Anna Kirk-Smith

57 Rhíannon - Birth of Pryderi
Sheila Knapp-Fisher
30˝ x 22˝ gouache on paper

I have been exploring the stories of ancient Welsh mythology collected together under the title "The Mabinogion" - The English translation and am absorbed in the emotions expressed between Gods and Humans in that moment of time. I continue to paint wild flowers and use gouache paint on paper.

Sheila Knapp-Fisher

58 The Holy Day Maker
Buzz Knapp-Fisher
1999

59 A New Invasion
Buzz Knapp-Fisher

Working in a Green Way for Fishguard. Art. Sciences, Environmental Advice and talk. 'The work I do has been described didactic in its nature with a sense of jest. My paintings and sculpture make a statement. Sometimes it's political. I also like making art just to bring happiness.'

Buzz Knapp-Fisher

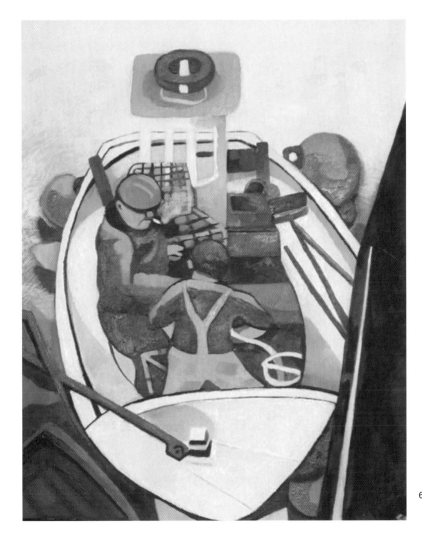

61 **Tenby Harbour**
Anne Gregson

60 **Porthgain**
Sarah Young
oil on canvas

My work is mainly inspired by the north Pembrokeshire landscape, which I explore through drawing anything that captures my attention. I then return home and begin to paint from the charcoal sketch and whilst painting (mainly in oils) I think about the spirit of the place and the essence of the subject matter, through working like this I believe the image becomes simpler but stronger.

Pembrokeshire means more to me than just beautiful scenery. As it is full of childhood memories and old stories that have been passed down to me by family members and local characters, memories that add to the mood and spirit of the place.

Sarah Young

62   M72
Geoff Yeomans
60″ x 138″ oil on canvas (triptych) 1995

Geoff Yeomans wanted to make powerful paintings so his work became life-sized and sometimes over life-size. The painted image became eidetic, not to fool the eye but to create a vivid representation to attract the viewer, a foothold from which anyone might approach other levels in the work.

'M72', the boat, was a material object that bore the marks of time with good grace. It is a metaphor of anguished gritty resistance. It is evidence of energy expended against time and tide. It has it's own special beauty at the fag end of it's life.

64 **In Flight**
Katrina Head
gouache

63 **Snake Pipefish, Martins Haven**
Katrina Head
acrylic

65   **Rock of Ages**
Graham Brace
35 x 63 cms pastel pencil, coloured pencil, gouache

66   **Dancing Trees**
Graham Brace
33 x 33 cms
coloured pencil, watercolour, gouache

67   **Haroldston Church**
Graham Brace
38 x 40 cms
coloured pencil, chalk pastel, gouache

My pictures are very representational - almost photographic. Although I use a mixture of media including chalk pastels, watercolour and gouache, I work predominantly in coloured pencils. Coloured pencils give me enormous control over the marks that I make to achieve a high degree of detail. A combination of dissolving, blending, rubbing out and scratching also helps to add effect. I will draw anything that interests me visually, be it landscape, seascape or perhaps a small feature within a landscape. It could be a particular quality or phenomenon of light, tree shapes, stone arrangements or cloud formations... whatever. Pembrokeshire and in particular the countryside and estuarine scenery around Llangwm where I live, will always provide more than enough ideas and inspiration.

Graham Brace

68 **The Blue Lagoon**
Andrea Kelland
oil

Andrea Kelland's paintings of land meeting sea have a sense of peace, history and now. Her work is almost entirely concerned with the Pembrokeshire coast: an immense source of material. She strives to retain the subjects own poetry or drama, painting grand and eroding cliffs, the headlands pounded and shaped by seas, wave-shaped bays, rocky caves, pools and tidelines.

International award winning artist Andrew G Bailey is constantly inspired by the beautiful coastline and countryside of Pembrokeshire where he lives. 'It is the western light that makes this area a magical place', says Andrew. 'The everchanging moods of the sea, the dramatic skies and the ancient sites of early settlers add an atmosphere to the place and help create views that are just crying out to be painted.'

Andrew Bailey

69   Early Morning Mists - Cardigan Road
Andrew Bailey
52 x 33 cms watercolour

70   Solva Harbour Mouth
Andrew Bailey
68 x 34 cms watercolour

71 Fisherman
Andy Davies
photograph

72 Grassholm
Andy Davies
photograph

73   **A la recherche du temps perdu**
Arthur Giardelli
mixed media relief construction

In my studio in the former school of Warren I make my relief construction from discarded things and materials. These constructions range in size from eight inches to 3 x 4 feet square. Many are based on drawings made of the sea and take three to four months to make. What I collect, and my drawings, revive my experiences among the rock pools, waves, mists, lights, storms and distances at the sea's edge. I have done the same for fields of wheat, for the last glow of sunlight seen from deep in the wood and for the sky at night.

I live near the wild Pembrokeshire coast where I draw the sea and shore in all weathers, direct from nature if at all possible.

Arthur Giardelli

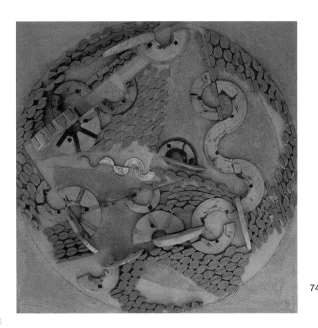

74   **Hub**
Arthur Giardelli
wood, sacking and brass, relief construction

75 Evening on the Beach
Bim Giardelli
fabric picture

David Jones worked for a while in the scriptorium of the Benedictine Monastery on Caldey Island. It is in the watercolours he painted there of the cliffs and the sea that he begins to use Impressionist colour for his play of light. He had been taught by Sickert and Hartrick who had known Gauguin and Van Gogh. He also had in mind '...that incomparable master Turner.' Here it is that he first describes in wave after wave the thrust of the tide and the enticing lure of the sea's face. He revisited Ynys Bŷr in 1931 and in 'The Reefed Place' showed how perilous the apparent haven of the shore could be.

In the same year, sitting with his back to the gas fire in a seaside bungalow in Portslade looking across the verandah to the sea's horizon, he had painted his vision of Manawydan's Glass Door, which in Celtic myth was in a palace on Gwales, now called Grassholm.

It is when you look from the distance of another time or place that you see what Pembrokeshire has done for artists who have lived or travelled here.

Arthur Giardelli, Extract from 'Pembrokeshire Painters' (May 1991).

76   Tree Stump
Nicola van Schie

'My personal approach divides my output into the celebration of the retinal excitement of the coastal images and the surrealistic approach to human and social issues.'

Philip Muirden

Nicola van Schie has exhibited paintings, original prints, sculptures and stone carvings. She works on abstracting initial observational objects, making a statement or creating an impression. She searches for the essence, discovers the quality, creating an environment to allow the image to expand outside its own space/disappear in its own surroundings.

77   Ghost Ship
Philip Muirden
6´ x 4´ oil on canvas

78   Harbour Entrance II (Entrance to Porth Clais Harbour)
Roy Ayres
72 x 53 cms watercolour and gouache

'The move to Pembrokeshire was the result of a deliberate effort to find an environment that would provide the impetus and the inspiration to re-start painting properly. I feel that whilst painting I am on a kind of journey of discovery. Something has started me off and I am prepared to end up with something quite different to the painting that was in my minds eye to begin with'.

Roy Ayres

79 **Home Before Dark**
Lynn Llewelyn Davies
mixed media

80 **Silhouette**
Lynn Llewelyn Davies
mixed media

I was born in 1947 but didn't start painting until 1986. I am self-taught but have learnt much from the work of the many talented artists in Pembrokeshire.

On moving to Pembrokeshire in 1990 I was inspired by the power and vastness of the sea and attempt to capture the changing light that affects the mood of this beautiful coastline.

Ruth Coulson

81 **Low Tide, Ricketts Head, Newgale**
Ruth Coulson
470 x 375 mm watercolour

82 St Govan's Head
Susan Sands
18˝ x 27˝ pastel and wash

83 Fruit and Flowers
Susan Sands
28˝ x 46˝ collage

Susan Sands has lived in India and London, but now works as a painter and printmaker in Wales, in a studio overlooking the River Cleddau.

She works in cycles, allowing the direct and sometimes accidental effects of printmaking to influence her painting and vice versa - a sort of 'ladder of experience' where one thing builds on another and sallies into collage and monoprinting are steps to a freer response in the subtle transparencies of water colour or bolder more sweeping applications of acrylic. She is aware of and welcomes constant change in her work.

84 **Into the light, Solva**
Heather Bennett
photograph

85 **Thrifts, Abermawr**
Heather Bennett
photograph

86 **Tenby Seagull**
Heather Bennett
photograph

87 **Venetian Carnival 1**
Raul Speek
oil on canvas

Raul Speek was born in Cuba in 1958 and came to the UK in 1991 following BBC Arena's programme on Cuba's young political artist. He has lived and worked in Pembrokeshire since 1996. His work is both abstract and figurative and is often further interpreted by music which he writes and performs. He has a gallery and open studio in Solva - open daily. For more information visit him there or see www.raulspeek.com.

Heather Bennett began printing her own work at the age of eleven in her father's darkroom. Moved to Pembrokeshire in 1996 where she has gloried in the beauties of Wales and how they can be re-created photographically in black and white and colour. Currently working on a book called 'Glimpses of Wales'. To see her work visit Raul Speek Gallery, Solva or see her web page www.heatherbennett.co.uk.

88   **Tenby**
Jake Sutton
22˝ x 30˝ charcoal 1994

89   **Boat and Rope, Tintern, Wales**
Jake Sutton
size charcoal 1996

90 Bosherston Lily Ponds - Wild Wales Series
Viv Tozer
oil

91 Fishguard Harbour
Daniel Lee Goff
watercolour

92 Rocks at Barafundle
Daniel Lee Goff
watercolour

It seems that Pembrokeshire is a place that captures people's hearts and as a watercolourist there is no better place to live and work.

From early morning sea mists and breathtaking sunsets, to the highly-charged atmosphere of the storm, Pembrokeshire's spectacular coastline provides me with an ever-changing source of inspiration.

Daniel Lee Goff

93   **Aberfelin**
Graham Hurd-Wood
oil

My paintings represent a personal interest in the activity of painting, most of my work is made in situ "out there" and in that sense it is a search for a direct connection, a contemporary view of an eternal subject. One thing is definite, the present is elusive - it always has been - as soon as it seems fixed its as good as over - history again. My objective is to make something of the moment to interest in equivalent so that others too can connect with the process of painting the physical world.

Graham Hurd-Wood

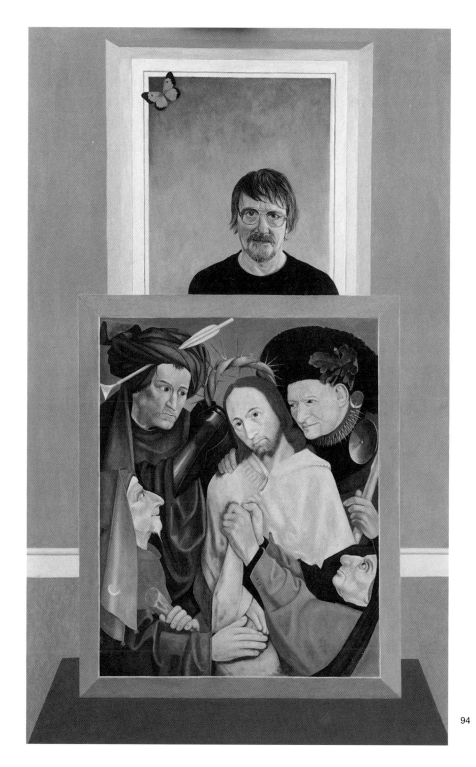

Tony Steele-Morgan's work is well known to many people and he is recognised as an accomplished painter and illustrator. He was trained in the traditional manner before the advent of free expression which seems to prevail in certain areas. To appreciate this, one has only to look at his most mature work to witness the influence of many of the 'Old Masters' - Hieronymous Bosch in particular.

94   Portrait of an incompetent forger
Tony Steele-Morgan

95 **Vessel in a storm**
Elizabeth Haines
acrylic

96 **The Deep Blue Sea, Solva**
Barbara Price
oil

97 The Minstrel
Perryn Butler
80 cms Portland Stone

98 Adam and Eve
Perryn Butler
55 cms Bathstone

'My carving is predominantly figurative. I am interested in the relationships and connections between people. The aim is to capture a moment of emotion, a timeless feeling in a solid, ancient material such as stone in which to portray serenity, the melding of lovers, discord, rage, in fact any emotion that people can experience. Studying the Mabinogion and other Welsh and Celtic mythology has been an enriching experience both from a huge sense of tribal belonging and just the sheer wonder of the stories and magnificence of the Gods and Goddesses.'

Perryn Butler

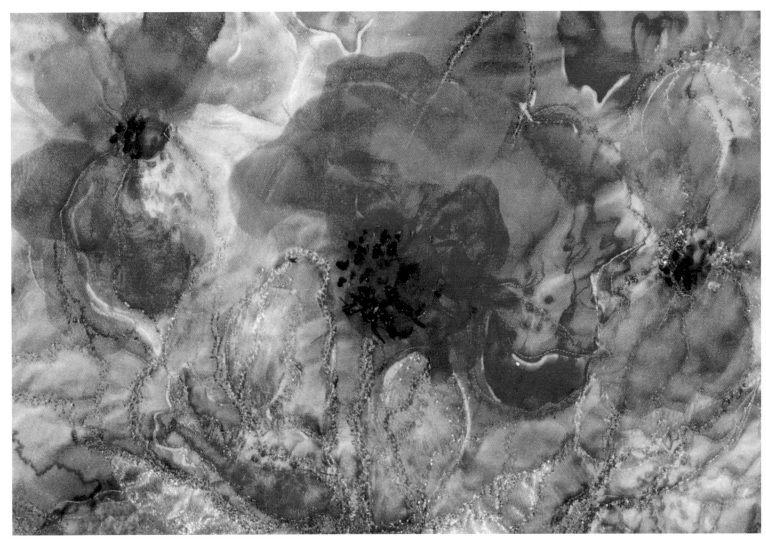

99 **A Touch of Silk**
Jan Hagan-Bossom
textiles

100 Evening
Rita Howlett
66 x 127 cm hand dyed dupion, satin and habotai silks.
Layered, cut, appliqued and machine embroidered

I have been living and working amidst the mountains and valleys of Wales for 20 years. The wildness of the scenery and the peacefulness that can be found in this beautiful country has influenced my work to such an extent that it is now unrecognisable from anything I produced whilst in Devon. I now only work with abstract forms, dyeing the silk myself to obtain the colours and textures I need for my layered, cut, appliquéd and machine embroidered hangings which are inspired by the deep valleys of Carmarthenshire and large skies of Pembrokeshire.

Rita Howlett

101 Trellis
Rita Howlett
53 x 64 cm hand dyed dupionsilk and string.
Layered, cut, appliqued and machine embroidered

102 Spring Brimming Sea
Daniel Backhouse
100 x 100 cms oil on board 2001

I've lived in Pembrokeshire for about 15 years. This place was a kind of revelation initially for all the usual reasons: changing light / sea / coast / season and enough left of itself, to reveal something of itself. Since then I've been led by it, currently to a place I do not recognise but I still feel its presence.

Daniel Backhouse

103 **Stackpole School Millennium Arch**
Robert Jakes

104 **Snake Fountain**
Robert Jakes
2.5m ceramic tile

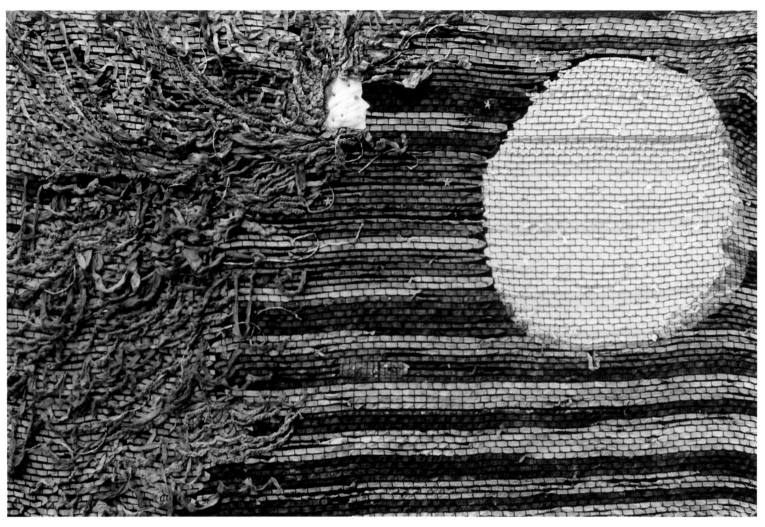

105 Cloths of Heaven
Diane Lucas

Diane Lucas specialises in Creative Textiles in 'building up', heavily textured surfaces through the multitude of techniques used, including weaving, crochet, embroidery and spinning. The work can be personal or huge community art projects. Diane works to commission, on site-specific community art projects and runs workshops and residential courses.

107 Moonrise Over Waves, South Pembrokeshire
Maurice Sheppard

106 Three Breton Trees
Maurice Sheppard

Maurice Sheppard was the first Welsh President of the Royal Watercolour Society (founded in 1804) and its youngest President since 1820. He was born at Llangwm in Pembrokeshire in 1947. Studying under Ronald Lowe at Haverfordwest Grammar School, he also attended a private class run by Mansel Adams, where his friends were Christopher Green and Ruby Pulinger. As a teenager he completed the mural of the 'Resurrection of the Earth' for the Communion of St Martin's Church. He represented Pembrokeshire youth as a scholar to the Eisteddfod Maldwyn at Newtown in 1965; he was sent because of his gifts in music composition and not as a linguist. Following an extensive art education, he has exhibited over 40 works in the years since 1971 at the Royal Academy in London at its Summer Exhibitions. He was awarded the Geoffrey Crawshay Memorial Travel Scholarship from the University of Wales, Cardiff in 1973 and travelled to Italy. His work has been purchased by seven museums and the image he created called 'The Golden Valley' was seen worldwide in Lord Richard Attenborough's movie 'Shadowlands'. In 2000 he was elected to the New English Art Club (founded in 1886).

108 Storm on Coast Path
Peter Green
watercolour and acrylic

Art captures the moment, the energy of the now. The presence of natural beauty, powerful landscapes and seascapes exposed to 'magical and transforming light' brings a sense of being and spirituality to the observer.

To interpret and represent these inspirational scenes either through painting or photography is a spiritual process and experience.

Peter Green

109 Caldey Island, Pembrokeshire
Peter Green
photograph

110 Sunset, Whitesands, Pembrokeshire
Peter Green
photograph

111 Celtic Horizon
Peter Green
photograph

112 Bowl
Phil McFadden

'Can it be that this piece is about the power of the waves and the wind, the constantly cycling action of give and take-back-and-forth currents gradually shaping the pebbles, the seashells, the rocks, the sand, the people - or is it about the female within the female whom I call Wife, a child who was born by knife - so that I saw a stark opening into this most natural world which I have long cherished and played a partner's role in, the eternal mystery of womb opening. Is it about the beginning and end of putting in and bringing forth a new life!? Maybe it's about the inner world which is always emerging to look at the outside, to show something of itself to the outside while bringing something of the outer back inside - to inform another exposure...'

Phil McFadden

113 The Green Bridge of Wales, Pembrokeshire
Graham Hadlow
watercolour

114 Parrog Beach, Pembrokeshire
Graham Hadlow
watercolour

For an artist, Pembrokeshire is a magical place offering as it does such a diversity of landscape within a relatively small area. The coastline with the ever changing moods of the sea, the quiet estuaries and attractive farms and villages are further enhanced by often rapid atmospheric changes. Together they provide scenes which can be dramatic or peaceful depending on the time of day and season. These variations are a constant source of inspiration.

Graham Hadlow

115 Bosherston
Rhoda Hodes
acrylic on canvas

Rhoda Hodes is a Pembrokeshire artist who lives at Freshwater East. She says, 'I find no challenge in copying exactly what is in front of me - I paint my emotional reactions to it. The colours are influenced by a South African childhood and are vibrant and clear. The movement of the paint is inspired by music, which is very important to my work.'

She paints mostly in acrylics on canvas and uses soft pastels. Subjects include dancers, musicians, fruit pickers, bathers and flower pieces, with an occasional Welsh landscape.

Pembrokeshire has never attracted a school of artists to the area as Cornwall has to Newlyn and St. Ives, but the nearest comparison is the art classes of Tenby given by E J Head. Artist Edward Head arrived in Tenby from Scarborough during the 1880's. Ten years later his art classes were attracting a large number of both local and seasonal residents, including the teenage siblings Augustus John and Gwen John. Nellie Powis Evans, Auguila Bowen and later Ida Jones were all enthusiastic students of his classes.

Pembrokeshire is able to claim that two of the most famous and talented female artists of the early twentieth century, Gwen John and Nina Hamnett, are from this county. But this claim is tinged with sadness at the fact that both had to pursue their lives as artists away from the area, and that neither, on leaving Pembrokeshire as young women, were rarely, if ever to return.

'You may travel the world over but you will find nothing more beautiful, it is so restful, so colourful and so unspoilt.' Augustus John, on Tenby, his birthplace.

116 Tenby Summer Time
Philip Sutton
36˝ x 36˝ oil on canvas 1995

Graham Sutherland first visited Pembrokeshire in 1834, describing Pembrokeshire as an area of "magical and transforming light". He has written of those early impressions saying "It was in this country that I began to learn painting".

These visits continued until 1947, returning some twenty years later to work on a film about his work inspired by his friend Pier Paulo Ruggerini.

It was a fateful return for he once again fell under the spell of Pembrokeshire - its forms, spaces and concentrations whose essence stimulated him both intellectually and emotionally.

It was in the early 70's that he decided he wanted to give something back - a selection of locally inspired work - to the county which had given him so much.

An introduction to the Hon. Hanning Philipps and his wife Lady Marian led to a later offer of the use of an annex to their Picton Castle home. It was less than a mile from his beloved, Picton estuary, the foreshore where he had already done so much drawing, and painting. So the idea of the Graham Sutherland Gallery was born.

Turner is regarded as the greatest nineteenth century landscape painter who, in his original use of light and colour was unmatched in the breadth of stylistic treatment and subject matter. In 1795 Turner made his first intensive tour of Wales, his intention being to collect material for typographical views and to draw picturesque scenery. During his tours of Wales, with the ever present sketchbook, he visited Tenby, Pembroke and St. Davids.

Pentigili - All the Way

Take 52 Pembrokeshire-based artists, one huge annual Welsh event - The National Eisteddfod of Wales - bring them together, and call it Pentigili.

The result was a successful fund-raising project never before seen in the county. It began five years before the Eisteddfod came to St. Davids, with a launch party in Narberth, and has since been exhibited all over Pembrokeshire. As well as selling some of the originals, five reproductions were made of each painting and these were on sale as well. The project proved very successful and profitable for the Eisteddfod, as well as giving thousands of people an opportunity to see the county's best artwork.

The word 'Pentigili' is a unique Pembrokeshire Welsh word, meaning 'The whole way.'

Cymerwch 52 o artistiaid sydd yn byw yn Sir Benfro, un digwyddiad blynyddol Cymreig - Eisteddfod Genedlaethol Cymru - unwch y ddau a'i alw yn 'Pentigili'.

Canlyniad hyn oedd prosiect llwyddiannus iawn na welwyd o'r blaen yn y sir. Dechreuwyd hyn bum mlynedd cyn i'r Eisteddfod ddod i Dyddewi, gyda pharti i lawnsio'r prosiect yn Arberth. Oddiar hynny, mae'r lluniau wedi eu harddangos dros y sir. Yn ogystal â gwerthu rhai o'r lluniau gwreiddiol, argraffwyd pump atgynhyrchiad o bob llun a gwerthwyd rhain hefyd. Roedd 'Pentigili' yn siawns dda i filoedd o bobl weld gwaith arlunio gorau'r sir, a ffordd unigryw i wneud arian i'r Eisteddfodd.

Mae'r gair 'Pentigili' yn unigryw i Sir Benfro, ac yn cyfieithu i 'yr holl ffordd.'

Ruth Barker

Sandy Haven
Theo Whalley

Cymylau tyrfau - Druidstone
Thunderclouds - Druidstone
Ann Whalley

Carreg Coetan - Trefdraeth
Carreg Coetan - Newport
Jon Bennett

Des i chwilio am y gwanwyn
I came looking for the spring
David Tress

Storm uwchlaw Niwgwl
Storm over Newgale
Lynn Llewelyn Davies

India
Olivia Argent

Cadwyn ar y tywod - Trefdraeth
Chain on the sand - Newport
Jonathan Cramp

Machlud dross Wlad yr Iâ
Sunset over Iceland
Glesni Wynn Williams

Porthgain
George Yeomans

Y Ffenestr Gron - Plas yr Esgob
The Rose Window - Bishop's Palace
Rebecca Brinton

Y ddraenen wen - Caeriw
The Hawthorn Tree - Carew
Graham Brace

Yr haf yng Nghaerfai
Summer at Caerfai
Graham Hurd Wood

Lan Sergeants Lane
Up Sergeants Lane
John Knapp-Fisher

Cildraeth Sir Benfro
Pembrokeshire Cove
Andrea Kelland

Carn Ingli
Sally James

Pentre Ifan
Rod Williams

Castell Caeriw
Carew Castle
Arthur Giardelli

Alarch yn hedfan
Flying Swan
Charlotte Cortazzi

Gardd ger y môr - Sir Benfro
Garden by the sea - Pembrokeshire
Elizabeth Cramp

Barafundle
Robert Jakes

Clawdd Sir Benfro
Pembrokeshire hedge
Maurice Sheppard

Abereiddi
Jean Thomas

Glannau porffor
Purple coast
Linda Norris

East Angle
Vanessa Pearson

Llwyni drain yn cydio
Thorn trees clasping
Elizabeth Haines

Aros
Waiting
Lynne Crompton

Abereiddi
Ozi Rhys Osmond

Porthgain
Buzz Knapp-Fisher

Bradychu Arianrhod
Arianrhod betrayed
Sheila Knapp-Fisher

Tirlun Cymreig o'r Canol Oesoedd
Mediaeval Welsh landscape
Martin Griffiths

Y Bowlen Tseineaidd
The Chinese bowl
Bim Giardelli

Yr hen gwch - Abereiddi
The old boat - Abereiddi
Alun Davies

Bale Draughsif
The Draughsif Ballet
Royston Hopson

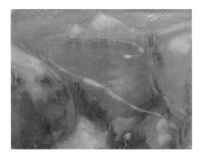

Cilfach
Inlet
Roy Ayres

Ar ymyl y cefnfor
At the ocean's edge
John Addyman

Bragdy plisgyn wy
Eggshell brewery
Ben Lloyd

Dafad fynydd yn y glaw
Mountain sheep in the rain
Denis Curry

Y twr
The Tower
James Campbell

Abereiddi
Sarah Young

Goleuni'r bore - Traeth Marloes
Morning light - Marloes sands
Marlene Barker-Williams

Pyllau golau leuad - Dinbych-y-Pysgod
Moonlit pools - Tenby
Graham Hadlow

Ymrafael morol
Marine mêlée
Anna Kirk-Smith

Rhwd
Corrosion
Goeff Yeomans

Aberfelin
Cherry Pickles

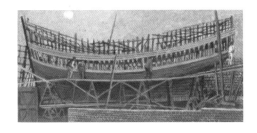

Adeiladu cwch
Boat building
Philip Muirden

Ystafell â golygfa
Room with a view
Tony Steele-Morgan

Goleuni'r bore - Y Preselau
Morning light - Preseli
Monica Groves

Carnedd Meibion Owen
Josh Partridge

Tremarchog
Penny Jones

Directory of Artists

The number reference after the artist or gallery refers to works featured in the book.

1. Apple Tree Gallery
Yvonne Mannings
Pen-y-Dre, The Ridgeway, Saundersfoot,
Pembrokeshire SA69 9JE
Tel & Fax 01834 813734
Opening times: Easter to Christmas 10.30am to 5pm or at other times by appointment.

2. Art Matters
South Parade, Tenby SA70 7DG
Tel 01834 843375
www.artmatters.org.uk

3. Roy Ayres (78)
5 Wades Close, Holyland Road,
Pembroke SA71 4BN
Tel 01646 622860

4. Daniel Backhouse (102)
3 Rhos Y Cae Rau, St Nicholas,
Goodwick SA64 0LB
Tel 01348 891317

5. Andrew G Bailey (69, 70)
Studio: 22 Heritage Park, Haverfordwest,
Pembrokeshire SA61 2QF
Tel/Fax 01437 762257
Access sample images on internet
www.axisartists.org.uk
Gallery: The Gallery, 23 Riverside Quay,
Haverfordwest Tel 01437 766889

6. David Bellamy (13, 14,)
Jenny Keal (15, 16, 17)
Maesmawr, Aberedw, Builth Wells,
Powys LD2 3UL
Tel 01982 560237
Email DAJbellemy@aol.com
www.DavidBellamy.co.uk
David Bellamy was born and brought up in Pembrokeshire. He mainly specialises in mountain and wild coastal scenes and has written 9 books illustrated with his paintings.

Five films on watercolour painting by David have been produced by APV Films of Chipping Norton. He also runs watercolour courses in Britain and overseas.
Through painting and writing he endeavours to bring about a greater awareness of threats to the natural environment. He is patron of the Marine Conservation Society's Seas for Life Appeal. David has been featured on radio and television in numerous programmes, including his television series "Painting Wild Horses".

7. Graham Brace (65, 66, 67)
Guildford House, Butterhill, Llangwm,
Haverfordwest, Pembrokeshire SA62 4JP
Tel 01437 891580
Email grahambrace@btinternet.com
www.grahambrace.com

8. Wendy Brickle
111 High Street, Pembroke Dock,
Pembrokeshire SA72 6PE
Tel 01646 686982

9. Perryn Butler (97, 98)
16 Goat Street, Haverfordwest,
Pembrokeshire SA61 1PXY
Tel 01437 767869
Email perryn.butler@btopenworld.com

10. John Cahill (33, 34)
The Harbour Gallery, 1 St Julian Street,
Tenby, Pembrokeshire SA70 7AY
Tel 01834 842370
www.tenbyharbourgallery.co.uk

11. Ruth Coulson (81)
Bryn Hedydd, Caerfarchell,
Nr Solva SA62 6XE
Tel 01437 721325

12. Denis Curry
Artist/Sculptor
Studio: Fron, Llanycefn, Clynderwen,
Pembrokeshire SA66 7XT
Tel Maenclochog 01437 532313

13. Andy Davies (71, 72)
1 Murchin Cottages, Marloes,
Haverfordwest, Pembrokeshire SA62 3BS
Tel 01646 636627

14. Helen Elliott (1)
Tollgate House, Carmarthen Road,
Newcastle Emlyn, Carmarthenshire
SA38 9DA
Tel 01239 711735
Email Elliot@elli8.fsnet.co.uk

15. Emyrs Art Supplies
Oriel Emyrs Gallery
8-10 Woods Row, Carmarthen SA31 1BX
Tel 01267 237147
15 High Street, Haverfordwest SA61 2BW
Tel 01437 779646
www.emyrsart.co.uk
Proprietors Tom and Glenys Learmonth
Art shops in Carmarthen and Haverfordwest, gallery in Haverfordwest, workshops and Summer Schools Programme.

16. The Gallery at Glanhelyg
Kath Sapey & Mike Williamson
Glanhelyg, Llechryd, Cardigan SA43 2NJ
Tel (Mike) 01239 682482
(Kath) 01239 682119
Email kathsapey@onetel.net.uk or
mike.williamson2@ntlworld.com
www.geocities.com/mike_williamson_uk
Opening times: Daily 10am - 6pm.

17. The Gallery at St Brides
St Brides Hotel, St Brides Hill,
Saundersfoot, Pembrokeshire, SA69 9NH
Tel 01834 812304
Fax 01834 811766
Email mail@thegalleryatstbrides.co.uk
www.thegalleryatstbrides.co.uk
Opening times: open all year 9am to 9pm.

18. Bim Giardelli (10, 12, 75)
Arthur Giardelli (8, 9, 11, 73, 74)
The Golden Plover Gallery, Warren,
Pembroke, Pembrokeshire
Tel 01646 661201

19. Daniel Lee Goff (91, 92)
Watercolourist
*23 Keats Grove, Priory Park, Haverfordwest,
Pembrokeshire SA61 1RY
Mobile 07989 225834*

20. Peter Green (108, 109, 110, 111)
*Bangeston, Angle, Pembrokeshire SA71 5AH
Tel 01646 641348
Mobile 07881 808246
Email celtichorizons@btinternet.com
www.celtichorizons.co.uk*

21. The Greenhalgh Studio
(20, 21, 22, 23)
Landscapes by Annabel Greenhalgh
Original work, Limited edition prints, Cards
*Llandaff Cottage, Melinau, Lampeter Velfrey,
Narberth, Pembrokeshire SA67 8TJ
Tel 01834 831633*

22. Anne Gregson (61)
Jo Davies
*Little Wedlock Gallery, Gumfreston, Tenby,
Pembrokeshire SA70 8RB
Tel 01834 845868*

23. Jan Gregson (36)
*Ferry Wood House, Pembroke Ferry,
Pembrokeshire SA72 6UD
Tel 01646 682364*

24. Graham Hadlow (113, 114)
*Nant-Oer, St. Florence, Nr Tenby,
Pembrokeshire SA70 8LN
Tel 01834 871548*

25. Jan Hagen-Bossom (99)
Textile Artist
*Vale Farmhouse, Vale Road, Houghton,
Milford Haven, Pembrokeshire SA73 1NW
Tel 01646 601073*
'Large colourful and abstract flower studies,
some incorporating her her own hand-dyed silk
threads and fabrics. Inspired by the beauty of
Pembrokeshire and her garden'.

26. Elizabeth Haines (95)
*Bryn Morris, Rhosfach, Clynderwen,
Pembrokeshire SA66 7QN
Tel 01437 532498*
I have lived in Pembrokeshire since 1968,
working as an illustrator, painter, writer, teacher
and farmer. The landscape and dwellings of
both west Wales and France appear in much of
my work and whilst being in the tradition of the
British Romantic school as well as early 20th
European art, my painting has been described
as mythological and dreamlike, depicting 'other
places'.
I exhibit in Cardiff, London and Bristol as well
as my studio at Bryn Morris. My work is in
many collections including the National Library
of Wales and the Contemporary Art Society for
Wales. In 1987 I was Artist in Residence at the
National Eisteddfod, and in 2001 was awarded
a Ph.D. in the Philosophy of Aesthetics at the
University of Wales, Lampeter.

27. Harbour Lights Gallery
Porthgain
Framework, bespoke framers and gallery.

28. Katrina Head (63, 64)
*1 Bridge Street, Hakin, Milford Haven,
Pembrokeshire SA73 3LT
Tel 01646 693017
Email katrina@headart.fsbusiness.co.uk*

29. Rita Howlett (100, 101)
Textile Artist
*Pencleppin, Blaenwaun, Whitland,
Carmarthenshire SA34 0JB
Tel 01994 448601
Email rita@stevehowlett.com*

30. High Seas Gallery (35)
David Morgan
*8 The Norton, Tenby SA70 8AA
Tel/Fax 01834 843611
Email jennifer@djpmorgan.freeserve.co.uk*
Home and principal gallery of the architect and
artist David J P Morgan who exhibits with The
Royal Society of Marine Artists.

31. Rhoda Hodes (115)
*102 Trewent Park, Freshwater East,
Pembrokeshire SA71 5LP
Tel 01646 672659*

32. Graham Hurd-Wood (2, 93)
*21 New Street, St Davids, Pembrokeshire
SA62 6SW
Tel 01437 720685*

33. Robert Jakes (103, 104)
Sculptor
*1 Home Farm Cottage, Pen-y-Wen,
Stackpole, Pembroke,
Pembrokeshire SA71 5DQ
Tel/Fax 01646 661485
www.tyrbwlch.freeserve.co.uk/robertjakes.htm*

34. Penny Jones
*6 King Street, Newport, Pembrokeshire
SA42 OPY
Tel 01239 820737
Mobile 07789 622420
Email pennyart50@hotmail.com*

35. Andrea Kelland (68)
*Long Lane, Amroth, Pembrokeshire
SA67 8PR
Tel 01834 831741*
Andrea's work can be seen in the Golden Sheaf
Gallery in Narberth (see listing) and at her
studio near Amroth, by appointment.

36. Anna Kirk-Smith (56)
*122 Churchfield Road, Acton,
London W3 6BY
Tel 0781 2602239
Email annakirk-smith@rca.ac.uk*

37. Buzz Knapp-Fisher (58, 59)
*The Field of Sound Office:
32 Main Street, Fishguard.
Tel 01348 874807
Home: St Gwendaf Cut, Llanwnda,
Goodwick, Pembrokeshire SA64 0HX
Tel 01348 874922
Email fieldofsound@btconnect.com*

38. John Knapp-Fisher (18, 19)

The Gallery, Trevigan Cottage, Croesgoch, Haverfordwest, Pembrokeshire SA62 5JP
Tel 01348 831374
Open Daily Easter to September
10.00am - 5.30pm
(Rest of the year by appointment).
Situated on the A487 between St. Davids and Fishguard.

39. Sheila Knapp-Fisher (57)

32 Main Street, Fishguard, Pembrokeshire, SA65 9HJ
Tel 01348 874731
Galleries exhibiting at:
Sessions Gallery, Newport, Pembrokeshire (Solo).
Permanent place at Harbour Lights Gallery, Porthgain, Pembrokeshire.

40. Lynn Llewelyn Davies (79, 80)

The Reading Room Gallery, Dale, Pembrokeshire
Tel 01646 636375
Mobile 07881 437964
Lyn Llewelyn Davies, working artist, was born on Anglesey but has lived in Pembrokeshire since 1947. Exhibits at a number of Galleries including the New Artists Gallery, St Davids and her own Reading Room Gallery.

41. Diane Lucas (105)

Textile Artist
Bwythyn Bach, 18 Port Lion, Haverfordwest, Pembrokeshire SA62 4JS
Tel/Fax 01646 601473

42. Phil McFadden (112)

51 Queen Street, Pembroke Dock SA72 6JF
Tel 01646 681859
Email dainesmcfadden@mac.com

43. Colin Morse

Priskilly Fawr Farm, Hayscastle, Haverfordwest, Pembrokeshire SA62 5QF
Tel/Fax 01384 840650
Opening times: Monday to Saturday 10am - 5.30pm, Sunday 12.30pm - 5.30pm.

44. Philip Muirden (77)

6 Hill Street, Hakin, Milford Haven, Pembrokeshire SA73 3LP
Tel 01646 692798
www.axisartists.org.uk
www.welshdrawing.

45. Oriel Albion Gallery

Nun Street, St Davids, Pembrokeshire SA62 6NU
Tel 01437 720120
Opening times: We are open throughout the year 9.30am to 5.30pm. Please verify during winter.

46. Oriel Glan y Môr

Margaret Jones and Beth Robinson
Market Square, Fishguard, Pembrokeshire SA65 9HA
Tel 01348 874787 & 01239 891485
Opening times: Mon to Sat 10am - 5.30pm

47. Oriel Linda Norris Gallery (41, 42)

Llywynon, Maenclochog, Clynderwen, Pembrokeshire SA66 7LB
Tel 01437 532580
Mobile 0777 3402129
Email linda@linda-norris.com
www.linda-norris.com
Gallery open times:
1st April - 31st October
Sunday, Monday, Tuesday 10am to 6pm. Other times by appointment.
1st November to 31st March
New Year week (1st -7th January) 10am to 6pm. Other times by appointment
Directions: The gallery is situated in the Preseli Hills in the heart of Pembrokeshire. The gallery is in the centre of Maenclochog village opposite 'Sarah's' Shop.

48. Vanessa Pearson

(45, 46, 47, 48, 49, 50)
Bay View, 4 The Point Road, Angle, Pembrokeshire SA71 5AS
Tel 01646 641468
Email vanessa.roy@talk21.com
www.axisartists.org.uk

49. Barbara Price (96)

Llanon Farm, Trefin, Haverfordwest, Pembrokeshire SA62 5AE
Tel/Fax 01348 837065
Mobile 07989 807402

50. Pebbles Yard Gallery & Espresso Bar

The Pebbles, Cross Square, St Davids
Tel 01437 720122
Opening times: Open 7 days a week.

51. Pembrokeshire Art & Framing

Wyon House, 9 Market Street, Haverfordwest, Pembrokeshire SA61 1NF
Tel 01437 779524
Email mail@pembsart.com
Opening times: Tuesday to Saturday 10am - 5pm, other times by appointment.

52. Susan Pomery-Wilks

1 Furzton Cottages, Stackpole, Pembrokeshire SA71 5BU
Tel 01646 682360
Pembrokeshire and Cornwall are my favourite venues because of my love for the sea. I use most mediums but specialise in acrylic impasto with with a pallet knife: colour, light, texture and atmosphere are my main objectives in painting.

53. Queens Hall Gallery

Lynne Morgan Crompton, High Street, Narberth, Pembrokeshire SA67 7AS
Tel 01834 861212
Fax 01834 861989
Email info@thequeenshall.com
www.thequeenshall.com

Opening times: All year Thurs, Fri and Sat 10am - 5.30pm, plus any access not in use for classes. Telephone to check.

54. Bob Reeves (5, 6, 7)
'Medina', Houghton, Milford Haven
Tel 01646 601133
A celebrated poet, painter and sculptor, Bob Reeves has become one of the county's most prolific artists - a truly multi-faceted talent. His work was once described by the late and much revered Professor Gwyn Alf Williams as 'That arresting fusion of the stark, the lyrical and the profane'. His unique vision and stunning execution mean that he has rapidly gained a reputation which has spread far beyond Wales and a following of collectors who value his work highly. One such is Dr. David Williams of Lambourne, Berkshire, an admirer who already has a number of Reeves' paintings in his collection. Dr Williams said 'He is able to translate his passions and communicate them through any medium. This sense of power combined with an innate sensitivity marks him as an artist of a rare and singular talent'.
It is the unique juxtaposition of sensitivity with what is on times a feeling of almost raw physical strength that has resulted in his oil paintings and sculpture being much sought after and featured in many collections in Britain and overseas.
Bob Reeves is Pembrokeshire born and continues to live and work in the hamlet of Houghton near Haverfordwest.

55. Rhosson House
5 Nun Street, St Davids, Pembrokeshire
Tel 01437 720386
Opening times: 10.30am to 5pm Monday to Saturday.

56. Gillian Richardson
Fine Art Photography
The Gallery, Fair Winds, Spittal,
Haverfordwest, Pembrokeshire SA62 5QT
Tel & Fax 01437 741311
Email gillmrichardson@aol.com
www.bestofruralwales.co.uk
Opening times: Mon to Fri 10am - 5pm variable during season only, please telephone first to avoid disappointment.

57. John Rogers (24, 25)
Peter's Lane Gallery, St Davids,
Pembrokeshire SA62 6HT
Tel 01437 720570

58. Susan Sands (82, 83)
The Longhouse, West Williamston, Kilgetty,
Pembrokeshire SA68 0TL
Tel/Fax 01646 657381
Email susan@sands.demon.co.uk

59. Sawyer Signs Gallery
The London Road Mall, Pembroke Dock,
Pembrokeshire
Tel 01834 814732 / 07990 916974
Opening times: 10am to 5pm Monday to Saturday

60. Nicola van Schie (76)
Old Bakery Cottage, Kensington Street,
Goodwick, Pembrokeshire SA764 0AL
Tel 01348 875420
Email nicole.vans@virgin.net

61. Maurice Sheppard PPRWS MA(RCA)
(106, 107)
Mole Bridge Cottage, 14 Apsley Street,
Rusthall Common, Tunbridge Wells,
Kent TN4 8NU
Tel 01892 513405

62. Raul Speek Gallery (87)
Heather Bennett Photographic
(84, 85, 86)
The Old Chapel, Main Street, Solva,
Pembrokeshire SA62 6UU
Tel 01437 721907
Email heather@heatherbennett.co.uk
www.raulspeek.com
www.heatherbennett.co.uk

63. St Davids Studio Gallery
14 Nun Street, St Davids, Pembrokeshire
SA62 6NS
Tel/Fax 01437 720648
Opening times: Open Bank Holidays & Wed to Sun (March to early January). Also open on Tues during July & August.

64. Tony Steele-Morgan (94)
30 City Road, Haverfordwest,
Pembrokeshire SA61 2ST
Tel 01437 764504

65. Mrs Alex Steele-Morgan
Illustrator
15 Goat Street, Haverfordwest,
Pembrokeshire
Tel 01437 762903

66. Philip Sutton (43, 44, 116)
Jacob Sutton (88, 89)
Claude Sutton
3 Morfa Terrace, Manorbier, Pembrokeshire.

67. Simon Swinfield (53, 54, 55)
Landscape and Maritime Artist
The Chapel by The Sea Gallery, The Chapel
House, Nolton Haven, Haverfordwest,
Pembrokeshire SA62 3NH
Tel 01437 710761
www.simonswinfield.com
Simon trained extensively in art and design, achieving his masters degree in Leicester.

 ### 68. Tenby Museum and Art Gallery Amgueddfa ac Oriel Gelf Dinbych-y-Pysgod
Castle Hill, Tenby, Pembrokeshire,
Wales SA70 7BP
Tel/Fax Ffon/Ffacs 01834 842809
Email/Ebost tenbymuseum@hotmail.com

69. Viv Tozer (90)
27 Brynteg, St Davids SA62 6SQ
Tel 01437 721888

70. The Naomi Tydeman Gallery
(29, 30, 31, 32)
Cobb Lane, Tenby, SA70 7AR
Tel 01834 845540
Opening times: Easter to New Year everyday 10am - 5pm, closed January - March.

71. Ann Whalley NDD, ATD, SWA (51)
Theo Whalley (52)

Haroldston House, Haverfordwest,
Pembrokeshire SA61 1UH
Tel 01437 762611
Fax 01437 769034
Email apwhalley@paint-away.freeserve.co.uk
or tjwhalley@paint-away.new.labour.org.uk

In her own work Ann is concerned with defining a response, emotional or intellectual more than an exact reproduction of a scene - a case of using, not copying. Using various techniques and an innovative use of materials, in the belief that the means justifies the end and that painting is hard enough in itself without being bound by the limitations of any one media.
Ann and her husband Theo recently opened their magnificent new studios with large gallery space at their home, for painting weekends and weekly residential courses for individual artists and painting groups.

72. Claudia Williams (26)
Gwilym Prichard (27, 28)

5 Picton Road, Tenby,
Pembrokeshire SA70 7DP
Tel 01834 849015

73. Gwyn Cecil Williams (3, 4, 38)
Maggie Driscoll Williams (37, 39, 40)

Ossg Fine Art, The Old Smithy, Bethlehem,
Cardigan Road,
Haverfordwest, Pembrokeshire SA62 5QL
Tel 01437 731398
www.ossgfineart.co.uk

74. Workshop Wales Gallery

Manorwen, Fishguard,
Pembrokeshire SA65 9QA
Tel 01348 891619

Workshop Wales Art Gallery, established in 1970 is Pembrokeshires oldest mixed exhibition gallery set in beautiful countryside just outside Fishguard. The gallery shows works by local, national and international artists. Watercolours, oils, woodcarving, leatherwork ceramics and bronzes are all on show in the exhibition spaces. A chance to walk around the sculpture garden should not be missed.
Artists of particular interest are local painter John Cleal and sculptor Mitch Cleal both of whom work in a variety of media within their fields, to international acclaim. Also noteworthy

John Cleal

are David Humphreys, Mike Scott and Alice Tennant, all of whom are regular contributors to the Gallery.
The Gallery is open March 1st-31st October daily. Closed Mondays.

75. Geoff Yeomans (62)

Falling Stones, Long Lane, Amroth,
Pembrokeshire SA67 8PR
Tel 01834 831741
Also on www.britart.com

Geoff Yeomans trained as an easel painter. Still life became the focal point of his working pattern. But traditional still life has little relevance in our times. Violins, fruit and flowers reveal a nostalgia for a life that probably did not exist.
His work had to be of now! The sight of a wrecked car on a breaker's stack is as much a memento mori as a skull in a Dutch still life.
The rusting side of a ship is as transient as a fallen petal or spilled wine.

76. Sarah Young (60)

Bryn Gwyn, 4 Ffordd y Felin, Trefin,
Haverfordwest, Pembrokeshire SA62 5AX
Tel 01348 831710
Email sarahyoung710@hotmail.com

I was born and bred in north Pembrokeshire and was educated in the local primary school at Croesgoch and then went on to St. Davids secondary school, after which I studied art and design at Carmarthen College of Art and Technology (1989-1991). After completing my foundation course at Carmarthen I went on to do a Fine Arts degree at Aberystwyth University (1992-1995).

77. West Wales Arts Centre

16 West Street, Fishguard, Pembrokeshire
SA65 9AE
Tel 01348 873867
http://home.btconnect.com/WEST-WALES-ARTS

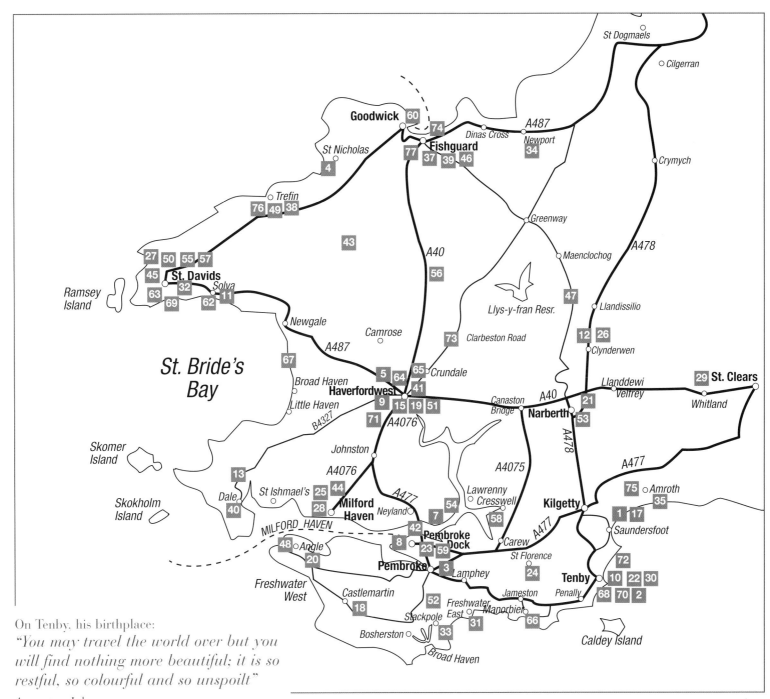

St Dogmaels

Cilgerran

Goodwick **60**

74 Dinas Cross *A487* Newport **34**

St Nicholas

4

77 **Fishguard** **37** **39** **46**

Crymych

Trefin

76 **49** **38**

Greenway

43

A40

Maenclochog

27 **50** **55** **57**

56

A478

45 **St. Davids**

63 **32** Solva

69 **62** **11**

47 Llandissilio

Ramsey
Island

Llys-y-fran Resr.

Newgale

A487 Camrose

73 Clarbeston Road

12 **26**

Clynderwen

*St. Bride's
Bay*

67

5 **64** **65** Crundale

Llanddewi   **29** **St. Clears**
Velfrey

Broad Haven **Haverfordwest** **41**

Canaston *A40* Whitland

Little Haven **9** **15** **19** **51** Bridge **Narberth** **21**

B4327 **71** *A4076* **53**

Skomer
Island

Johnston

A4076 *A4075* *A477*

13

Lawrenny
Cresswell Kilgetty **75** Amroth

Dale St Ishmael's **25** **44** **35**

28 **54** **58** **1** **17**

Skokholm
Island **40** **Milford
Haven** Neyland **7** *A477* Saundersfoot

MILFORD HAVEN **42** Carew *A477* **72**

48 Angle **8** **Pembroke
Dock** St Florence **10** **22** **30**

20 **23** **59** **24** **Tenby** **68** **70** **2**

Pembroke **3** Lamphey Jameston Penally

Freshwater
West Castlemartin **52** Freshwater
East Manorbier **66**

18 Stackpole **31** Caldey Island

Bosherston **33**

Broad Haven

On Tenby, his birthplace:
*"You may travel the world over but you
will find nothing more beautiful; it is so
restful, so colourful and so unspoilt"*
Augustus John

87

Craft Directory

= Member of the
Pembrokeshire Craftsmen's Circle

 = Member of
Pembrokeshire Craft Makers

1. Acres Beach Gallery
New Road, Newport, Pembrokeshire SA42 OSY
Tel & Fax 01239 820851
Opening times: Easter to 30th September, Monday to Thursday 10am - 4pm, but closed 7th - 25th June.

2. Ashera Pottery and Crafts
Ashera Pottery, Trallwyn, Mynachlogddu, Pembrokeshire SA66 7SE
Tel 01994 419278
Email trallwyn@clara.co.uk
www.home.clara.net/trallwyn/

3. Avondale Glass
Carmarthen Road, Kilgetty, Pembrokeshire SA68 0YA
Tel 01834 814278 & 813345
Opening times: Summer Season, Glassmaking: Mon, Tues, Thurs, Fri 9am to 2pm, Wed 9am to 1pm. Craft Shop: Mon to Fri 8am to 4pm, Sat 8am to 1pm.

4. Lillian Barker
35 Millfields Close, Kilgetty, Pembrokeshire SA68 0SA
Tel 01834 813882
Hand Crafted traditional Rag Dolls.

5. David Beattie
Etchings
Paisley Villa, Llandygwydd, Cardigan SA43 2QT
Tel 01239 682649
Email david@original-etchings.co.uk

Opening times: April to October - Monday to Friday 10am to 4pm
Closed Wednesday. Turn off from A484 (signposted Llandygwydd).
Gallery situated 500 yds up the village road opposite the phonebox.

6. Jill and Massemo Bissenden
Toys
Unit 7, Small Business Centre, Brodog Court, Fishguard, Pembrokeshire SA65 9NT
Tel 01348 875516

7. Blueberry Angoras
Ffynnon Watty, Moylegrove, Nr Cardigan SA43 3BU
Tel 01239 881668
Opening times: Open all year round Sunday to Friday inclusive 10am - 5.30pm, Saturday 2pm - 5.30pm.

8. Bosanquet
Hole in the Wall, Bridge Street, Haverfordwest, Pembrokeshire SA61 2AD
Tel 01437 769178
Opening times: Tuesday to Saturday 10am - 5pm.

9. Richard and Fran Boultbee
The Slate Workshop
Pont Hywel Mill, Llangolman, Clunderwen, Pembrokeshire SA66 7XJ
Tel/Fax 01994 419543
Email dothebiz@slate-workshop.co.uk
www.slate-workshop.co.uk

Opening times: Monday to Saturday 9.00am to 5.30pm Sunday 10am to 4pm. Phone first in winter. 1.5 miles from Efailwen on A478 and 4 miles from Maenclochog on B4313.
The Slate Workshop designs and makes high quality items in Welsh slate, working from the renovated 18th century corn mill, beside the Eastern Cleddau River, since 1985. Specialising in fine lettering and taking inspiration from the beautiful Pembrokeshire surroundings and from Celtic themes, the Slate Workshop make nameplates and numbers, sundials, commemorative plaques and memorials.
Richard creates his acclaimed curving sculptures from the heather purple slate of Penrhyn, the blue-black of Corris and the grey-green slate of Pembrokeshire. Individually designed and hand-made plates and vases, unique bookends, clocks, barometers, cheeseboards and tableware can also be found in the showroom.

10. Paul Brant
Primrose Cottage, Pill Parks Way, Llangwm, Nr Haverfordwest, Pembrokeshire SA62 4HT
Tel 01437 891572
Email palabrant@lineone.net
Unique one-off wooden boxes, tables and small furniture.
Opening times: Best to phone first; visitors welcome anytime.

11. Carol Brinton Thomas
10 Hean Close, Saundersfoot, Pembrokeshire SA69 9AD
Tel 01834 812958
Unique hand thrown pottery individually glazed and decorated in relief with daffodils or local scenes.

12. Kevin and Polly Brown
Clean Slate
9 Pembroke Ferry, Pembroke Dock, Pembrokeshire SA72 6UD
Tel 01646 621958
Mobile 07989 296953
Mirrors made from Welsh Slate - Decorative functional or fun.

13. Brychan Yard

Upper Frog Street, Tenby, Pembrokeshire
SA70 7JD
Tel 01834 842971 or 01834 871526
Opening times: Open 10am to 6pm Summer Season to Easter. Phone winter hours to avoid disappointment.

14. Caerwen Arts Studio

Caerwen, Glandwr, Hebron, Whitland,
Carmarthenshire SA34 OUA
Tel 01994 419537
Opening times: Weds, Thurs, Fri, Sun and bank holidays 10am - 5.30pm Easter to 1st October. For other times please telephone.

15. John and Victoria Jewellery

Ydlanddegwm, Llechryd, near Cardigan
SA43 2PP
Tel/Fax 01239 682653
Email jewellery@johnandvictoria.co.uk
www.johnandvictoria.co.uk

Open May to September -
Monday to Thursday 10am to 5.30pm
Also open in December. From Cardigan take the A484 to Llechryd. Turn right and cross the river - continue on this road for 1.6 miles.
John and Victoria Callan have lived and worked in Pembrokeshire for 22 years. Drawn to the area by its natural beauty and dramatic landscape they felt that their business of designing and making gold and silver jewellery would thrive here.
John and Victoria, now joined in the business by their daughter Bryony, are constantly inspired by their surroundings and base many of their designs on natural forms and textures - the wild flowers of the hedgerow, tree forms and stones from the Preseli Hills, the rugged coastline and the ever-changing patterns of the sea.
Our contact details are as above and our workshop and showroom is as the address and open May to end of September and December, Monday to Friday 10am - 5.30pm.

16. Celtic Images

Gary Roberts, Ann Stubbs and Richard Hellon
Hilton Court Gardens, Roch, Haverfordwest,
Pembrokeshire SA62 6AE
Tel 01348 837116
www.celticimages.co.uk
Evocative art and Photography of Pembrokeshire.

17. Crafts and Crocks

104 Main Street, Pembroke, Pembrokeshire
SA71 4HN
Tel 01646 684826
Open all year.

18. The Creative Café

David & Surrey Hartshorn
Spring Gardens, Narberth, Pembrokeshire
SA67 7BT
Tel /Fax 01834 861651
Email info@thecreativecafe.freeserve.co.uk
www.thecreativecafe.co.uk
A hands-on ceramics studio café where you decorate your own unique ceramics in a relaxing environment. Suitable for all ages. Artistic skill is not essential. We have plenty of ideas - books, stencils, sponges and more, plus friendly and helpful staff. Wide range of ceramics to choose from (tiles, cups, plates, animal figures, house plaques,etc). Prices from £1.50, plus a small studio fee to cover costs of paints, glazing and firing. You can stay all day!
Items are ready for collection in 1-3 days (postal service available). Superb coffee/ cakes/snacks.

19. DG Interior Designs

Driftwood Painting
www.dginteriordesign@aol.com
'Last night the sea had swallowed up the trash, recycled, it returned along with fishy things and bits of boats, sea-sculpted driftwood, pitted corks and many more, from which she plucks her treasures from the shore.'

20. Dockside Gallery

The Old Sail Loft, The Docks, Milford
Haven, Pembrokeshire SA73 3AF
Tel 01646 696311
Fax 01646 696302
Email gallery@milford-docks.co.uk
Opening times: Open all-year round 11am to 4pm 7days a week.

21. Wendy Evans

Brynarfor, Cwmins, St Dogmaels, Cardigan
SA43 3HF
Tel 01239 614761

22. Les Ford

Turned Wood
Dôl y Frenni, Boncath,
Pembrokeshire SA37 0JS
Tel 01239 841418 Fax 01239 841808

23. Francis Ceramics

Llandre, Llanfyrnach,
Pembrokeshire SA35 ODA
Tel 01239 831657
Fax 01239 831857
Email francisceramics@lineone.net
Opening times: weekdays only 10am - 4.30pm. Other times by appointment - telephone for weekends and bank holidays.

24. Furious Fish

14 Market Square, Narberth,
Pembrokeshire SA67 7AU
Tel/Fax 01834 861722
Email sara@jewellerywales.com
www.jewellerywales.com
Opening Times: Easter to Christmas Tuesday to Saturday 10am - 5pm, January to April often open but please phone first.
Furious Fish is where Sara Lloyd-Morris can be seen making her own individual style of jewellery, mostly inspired by the shoreline.

25. Annette Gardener

The Barn, Mabsgate, St Ishmaels,
Pembrokeshire SA62 3TL
Tel 01646 636612
Jewellery and small pictures with figurative images of cats, sheep, sea-birds etc.

26. Gail Gauden

Blaengwrfach, Bancyfordd,
Llandysul SA44 4RY
Tel 01559 362604
Pressed flowers with watercolour.

27. The Golden Sheaf Gallery

25 High Street, Narberth, Pembrokeshire
Tel 01834 860407
Opening times: Open all year 9.30am to 5.30pm Monday to Saturdays
Innovative contemporary art, crafts, jewellery, gifts and cards.

28. Lyne Griffiths

Cupboards
Cartref, New Moat, Clarbeston Road,
Haverfordwest, Pembrokeshire SA63 4RQ
Tel 01437 532949

29. Harbour View Ceramic Cafe

3 Crackwell Street, Tenby, Pembrokeshire
Tel 01834 845968
Email info@ceramiccafes.co.uk
www.ceramiccafes.co.uk
Opening times: 10am till late.

30. Jim Harries

Woodturner
Siop Fach, Mathry, Haverfordwest,
Pembrokeshire SA62 5HB
Tel/Fax 01348 831379
Opening time: Shop open all year. Summer Monday to Friday 9.30am - 5.30pm, Saturday and Sunday 10am - 4pm.

31. Peter Harries

24 Waun Las, Scleddau, Fishguard,
Pembrokeshire SA65 9RB
Tel 01348 875484

32. Joanna Heneker

Llwynon, Newchapel, Boncath,
Pembrokeshire SA37 0EH
Tel 01239 841741
Email pjheneker@pjheneker.fsnet.co.uk
Wildlife and Botanic artist working in the medium of watercolour.

33. Sheila Hickey

Pottery
Venn Farm, Waterston Rd, Milford Haven
SA73 1DN
Tel/Fax 01646 690190
Email sheila.hickey@ntlworld.com
Opening times: Easter to December. 10am to 5pm. Closed Thursday.
Situated halfway between Waterston village and Milford Haven on the B4325. Signposted Venn Farm at entrance to lane.

34. Diana Hoare

Sculptor and Lettering Artist
6 New Street, St Davids,
Pembrokeshire SA62 6SN
Tel 01437 721585
Email stone@dianahoare.co.uk
Opening times: May to end September - Tuesday to Thursday 10am to 4pm. The shop is on the New Street in the centre of St Davids. Workshop open by appointment only.

35. Steve Howlett

Woodturner
Penclippin, Blaenwaun, Whitland,
Carmarthenshire SA34 0JB
Tel 01994 448601
www.stevehowlett.com
Opening times: Tues, Wed, Thurs only, Easter to 30th September 11am - 1pm and 2pm 4.30pm. At all other times by appointment.

36. Elissa Hudson

Upper Swanswell, Broad Haven,
Haverfordwest, Pembrokeshire SA62 3TY
Tel 01437 781431
Practical and pretty fabric covered boxes and gifts in a range of styles, shapes and sizes.

37. Juanita Humphris

Clettwr Jays
Clettwr View, Capel Dewi, Llandysul,
Ceredigion SA44 4PP
Tel/Fax 01559 362056
Email clettwr.jays@lineone.net
Papier Mâché with a sense of fun.

38. Inhouse Quilting

2 Water Street, Narberth, Pembrokeshire
SA67 7AT
Tel 01834 869011
Email d.norcross@lineone.net
Margaret takes on commissions from wall hangings to full sized quilts. Quilts with individual designs are made up using a number of techniques from bleaching, piecing, manipulating the cloth to wadding and cloth folding before sewing. Pembrokeshire shoreline, marine life, skies and stunning scenery provide the inspiration.

39. Jellyegg

The Old Town Hall, High Street, Narberth,
Pembrokeshire SA67 7ER
Tel 01834 860061
Opening Times: Open all year 9.30am to 5.30pm Monday to Saturday.

40. Rick Leech

111 James Street, Llanelli, SA15 1EB
Tel 01554 759604
Glass Engraving also carved wood - walking sticks.

41. Phillippa Lewis
Little Haven Pottery
Berry Cottage, Little Haven,
Haverfordwest SA62 3UG
Tel 01437 781015
Email littlehavenpottery@supanet.com
Originally designed and attractively decorated functional stoneware pottery in blue, white and green.

42. Carl March
41 St Leonards Avenue, Crundale,
Haverfordwest, Pembrokeshire SA62 4DW
Tel 01437 763505

43. Sylvie McCracken
Vine Cottage, Lampeter Velfrey, Narberth,
Pembrokeshire SA67 8UQ
Tel 01834 831115
Tiny hand-stitched collages - drawing with threads.

44. Melin Tregwynt
Tregwynt Mill, Castlemorris, Haverfordwest,
Pembrokeshire SA62 5UX
Tel Shop 01348 891288
Office 01348 891225
Fax 01348 891694
Email info@melintregwynt.co.uk
www.melintregwynt.co.uk

45. Narberth Pottery
2 Market Street, Narberth
Pembrokeshire SA67 7AX
Tel 01834 860732
Simon Rich and his daughter Bryony, are both acclaimed potters and Catherine, his wife, specialises in hand painted ceramics. They all produce a range of eyecatching pots, plates and dishes that have won acclaim far and wide. Simon's crystalline glazeware is of outstanding interest. He produces beautiful zinc crystals on pieces that come in all shapes and sizes Their showroom is behind a traditional shop front. In it you will find Bryony's dazzling fumed copper raku, subtle terrasigilata, glorious lapis lazuli ware and Catherine's unique gold, silver and enamelled lustre ware. It is an ideal place to choose a very special gift or personal treat.

The Rich family's skills have gained recognition throughout the UK, and their quality and unique style are known far and wide. Narberth Pottery occupies premises close to the centre of Narberth, just off the main square. Narberth, sited on a hill, is rich in history and well worth a leisurely visit, but even without the literary and historical associations it's well worth taking time to admire the Rich family's work; the pottery is open from 10.30 to 5.30 Monday to Saturday, with a short closure at lunchtime.

46. Shirley Norman
Calligraphic Cards
2 Holbrook Close, Broad Haven,
Haverfordwest Sa62 3JE
Tel/Fax 01437 781775
Mobile 07887 714507
Open any reasonable hour; phone first if travelling from a distance.

Take the B4341 Broad Haven road from Haverfordwest, turn first left after the Broad Haven sign, then first turning right. 'Designs often cover both front and back of the cards. Some bilingual: English with Welsh, Irish and Scots Gaelic, French and Latin. There are cards for most occasions, calligrams (where the words form the shape of the subject they describe), tongue twisters, music and Celtic stories. Produced wholly in Pembrokeshire, the cards leave for destinations throughout the UK and various parts of the world.

47. Oculus
19 Main Street, Solva SA62 6UU
Tel 01437 729082
Opening times: Open all year 11am to 4pm with additional opening April to October.

48. The Old Smithy Craft Centre and Gallery
Simpson Cross, Haverfordwest,
Pembrokeshire SA62 6EP
Tel 01437 710628
Opening times: 10am - 5.30pm Easter to end of October and weekend opening from mid November to Christmas.

49. Pembroke Castle Brass Rubbing Centre
Pembroke Castle, Pembroke,
Pembrokeshire SA71 4LA
Tel 01646 681510 / 684585
www.pembrokecastle.co.uk
Opening Times: Call to avoid disappointment.

50. Pembrokeshire Candle Centre
Trefelin, Cilgwyn, Newport,
Pembrokeshire SA42 0QN
Tel 01239 820470
Fax 01239 821245
Email cilgwyncandles@appleonline.net
www.pembrokeshirecandles.co.uk
Opening times: Easter to end of October, daily 11am - 5pm. November and December, daily 12noon - 4pm. Rest of the year - restricted opening times. Please ring if coming far.

51. Penally Pottery
Penally, Tenby, Pembrokeshire SA70 7PR
Tel 01834 843796
Peter Day has created hand modelled stoneware pottery pieces for some 25 years in his gallery overlooking the village green and Norman Church. The myths, magic and legends of Pembrokeshire are translated into sculptures, dragons, wizards, witches and fanciful castles are but a few of Peter Day's unique creations. He specialises in commissions to order, popular for special birthdays, anniversaries and retirements.

52. Preseli Mohair Centre

Dolau Isaf Farm, Mynachlogddu,
Clunderwen, Pembrokeshire SA66 7SB
Tel & Fax 01994 419327
Email vivlockton@tinyworld.co.uk
Opening times: May to September inclusive, usually open Tuesday to Friday 11am - 5pm. Restrictive opening thereafter and on agricultural show days. Please telephone if travelling any distance.

53. Julie Randell

Look Twice Originals
4 Woodland Crescent, Milford Haven,
Pembrokeshire SA73 1BZ
Tel 01646 699556
Hats for sport and leisurewear, for all the family; to order or 'off the peg'.

54. Red Herring

2 Hamilton Street, Fishguard,
Pembrokeshire SA65 9HL
Tel 01348 874178
Fax 01348 811675
Email shop@red-herrings.org
www.red-herrings.org
Opening times: Summer months 11am - 4pm. Closed Wednesdays. Winter times variable, ring to confirm on 01348 811362

55. Neil Richardson

Mobile 07790113176
Email rakurichie@mac.com
All of Neil's work is 'Raku' glaze fired. This method of achieving effects is extremely random and suits his approach to the throwing of his work which is spontaneous and with no two pieces alike. It enhances the special quality that Neil hopes to achieve in his finished work.

56. Jo and Leigh Rihan

Claybridge Cottage, Rickeston, Milford
Haven, Pembrokeshire SA73 3TG
Tel 01437 781923
Email rihan@tcp.co.uk
Woodturners and woodworkers - rounded Pembrokeshire wood in an unlimited number of shapes and sizes.

57. Tony Shell

Wood
12 Millfields Close, Kilgetty, Pembrokeshire
SA68 0SA
Tel 01962 867028

58. Riita Sinkkonen-Davies

Handweaving
Mathom House, Moorland Road, Freystrop,
Haverfordwest, Pembrokeshire SA62 4LE
Tel 01437 890712
Email riita@rasdavies.co.uk
www.rasdavies.co.uk
Opening times: Easter to October - Tuesday to Thursday 10am to 6pm
From Haverfordwest take Burton/Llangwm road. In Freystrop turn right and immediately right again onto Moorland road - third house on the left.
"The dramatic beauty of Pembrokeshire provides a constant inspiration for all my work. It is most obvious in my woven landscapes, that reflect the moods of the sea and coast or the changing seasons on Preseli Mountains."

59. Snail Trail Handweavers

Martin & Nina Weatherhead, *Penwenallt*
Farm, Cilgerran, Nr Cardigan,
Pembrokeshire SA43 2TP
Tel/Fax 01239 841228
Email martin@snail-trail.co.uk
www.snail-trail.co.uk
Opening times: Easter to September, generally Monday to Friday 10am - 1pm, 2pm - 5pm. If

travelling far please telephone first to avoid disappointment. By arrangement in winter.
'There is something of a Magic Land about Pembrokeshire. Deep valleys and strange rocky outcrops with little sign of the outside world. The light comes and goes in amazing intensity. I find inspiration from the colours all around and through the seasons.'
Martin Weatherhead has been running Snail Trail Handweavers since 1976 and has developed his own style of rug and fabric weaving. He has a particular interest in Ikat dyeing which gives a range of effects from bold to subtle. The technique allows large-scale designs and gives wonderful soft blends between areas of colour. All his work is unique and unrepeatable, though similar pieces can be made. Rugs, wallhangings, cushions, scarves and fabrics are available from the studio and exhibitions. Commissions are welcomed and Martin is able to match or complement existing colour schemes. He also makes tapestries and has re-created historical fabrics for museums. The studio holds residential and non-residential courses in weaving, spinning and dyeing from Easter to October.

60. Solva Pottery

Main Street, Lower Solva, Pembrokeshire
Tel 01437 720516
Opening times: Open virtually every day.
Please phone to confirm.

61. Solva Woollen Mill

Middle Mill, Solva, Haverfordwest,
Pembrokeshire SA62 6XD
Tel 01437 721112
Email enquiries@solvawoollenmill.co.uk
www.solvawoollenmill.co.uk
Opening times: Open all year Monday to Friday
9.30am - 5.30pm. Additional opening Easter to
end September Saturday 9.30am - 5.30pm,
Sunday 2pm - 5.30pm.

62. Stepaside Craft Village and Art Gallery

Pleasant Valley, Stepaside, Kilgetty,
Pembrokeshire SA67 8LN
Tel 01834 811686
Out of season 01834 811134
Fax 01834 811104
Email craftvillage@saundersfoot.co.uk
www.saundersfoot.co.uk/craftvillage
Opening times: Easter to end of September
11am to 5pm, Sundays 10am to 5pm Mon - Fri.
October 11am - 4pm.

63. Tecstiliau Tŷ Twt

Tŷ Twt, Heol y Farchnad,
Trefdraeth/Newport, Sir
Benfro/Pembrokeshire SA42 OPH
Tel & Fax 01239 821056
Opening times: All year Monday to Saturday
10am - 5pm.

64. Roy Thedvall

Artist Blacksmith
Castell, Crymych, Pembrokeshire
SA41 3QW
Tel/Fax: 01239 831959
Email roythedvall@hotmail.com
Open: Easter to October weekdays 11am to
5pm
Entrance to Castell is on the A478 between
PentreGalar and Crymych (approx 1.5 miles
south of Crymych).

65. Steve Thompson

Yet Wen, Newchapel, Boncath,
Pembrokeshire SA37 0HG
Tel/Fax 01239 841431
Email stevethompsondesigns@hotmail.com
Contemporary furniture in birch ply.

66. Mark Walford

Pottery
Troyan, Llanfyrnach,
Pembrokeshire SA35 0DA
Tel 01994 419566
Email potwrite@tesco.net
wwwmarkwalford.co.uk
With my partner Sue and our cats we make
crystal glaze vase and bowl forms. Open by
appointment only.

67. Moira White

Moriath Glass
Nant Cwmpengraig, Drefach, Velindre,
Llandysul, Carmarthenshire SA44 5HY
Tel 01559 371585
Vibrant hand-painted glass - goblets,
candleholders, bowls, vases and mirrors.

68. Wolfscastle Pottery

Maddy and Philip Cunningham
Wolfscastle Pottery, Wolfscastle,
Pembrokeshire SA62 5LZ
Tel/Fax 01437 741609
Email philcunningham@talk21.com
Creative Breaks in Pembrokeshire - Finding your
way with Clay. Exploring the Coastline. Climbing
and Abseiling. Surfing and Swimming. Yoga and
Meditation. Aromatherapy.
Situated in the St. Davids Peninsula, an unspoilt
corner of Wales, Wolfcastle Pottery is an ideal
place to come for a relaxing holiday. It has a
wild sunny climate, spectacular coastal
scenery, a profusion of wild flowers, an
abundance of wildlife, friendly people and a
leisurely pace of life. This small country pottery
is surrounded by meadows and is only a short
drive from the coast and the Preseli mountains.

69. The Wool Gallery

Llain Farm, Mathry, Haverfordwest,
Pembrokeshire
Tel 01348 837634
Opening times: Tuesday to Friday 10.30am -
5pm, Sundays 12pm - 4pm. January to end of
March open 12pm - 4pm Tuesday to Friday and
Sundays.

A selection of work by
members of the
Pembrokeshire Craft Makers

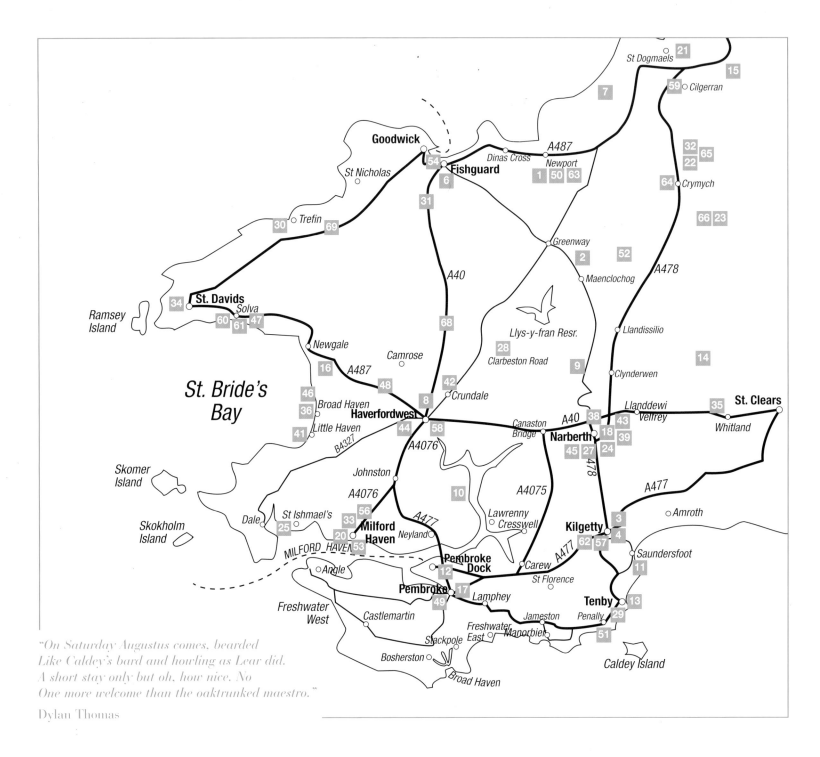

St Dogmaels 21

15

59 Cilgerran

7

32 65
22

64 Crymych

66 23

Goodwick

54
Fishguard
6

Dinas Cross

Newport
1 50 63

A487

St Nicholas

31

Greenway

A40

2 52

Maenclochog

A478

30 Trefin 69

St. Davids 34

Ramsey
Island

Solva
60 61 47

Newgale

16 A487

Camrose

48

42

68

Llys-y-fran Resr.

28

Clarbeston Road

9

Llandissilio

Clynderwen

14

St. Bride's
Bay

46
36 Broad Haven

41 Little Haven

B4327

Crundale

8

44 58

Haverfordwest

A4076

Canaston
Bridge

A40

38

Llanddewi
Velfrey

35 St. Clears

43

Whitland

18
Narberth
39

45 27 24

Skomer
Island

Johnston

A4076

10

A4075

478

A477

Skokholm
Island

Dale

St Ishmael's

25

33 56

20
53

Milford
Haven

Neyland

MILFORD HAVEN

Angle

Lawrenny
Cresswell

3

Amroth

Kilgetty
4

62 57

A477

Saundersfoot

11

Pembroke
Dock

12

Carew

St Florence

Pembroke 17

49

Lamphey

Castlemartin

Freshwater
West

Stackpole

Bosherston

Broad Haven

Freshwater
East

Jameston

Manorbier

Penally

Tenby 13

29

51

Caldey Island

*"On Saturday Augustus comes, bearded
Like Caldey's bard and howling as Lear did.
A short stay only but oh, how nice. No
One more welcome than the oaktrunked maestro."*

Dylan Thomas